Los Luceros

Los Luceros

New Mexico's Morning Star

By Michael Wallis
Photography by Gene Peach

Museum of New Mexico Press
Santa Fe

Starry skies over Casa Grande

For Suzanne, who introduced me to Los Luceros,
for John Lennsen, who made this book possible,
and for all those who protect and preserve Los Luceros

Water channel in the woods

Acknowledgments

THERE ARE MANY PEOPLE TO THANK for the incredible wealth of assistance I received during the researching and writing of this book. Their input and guidance were essential and greatly appreciated: John and Diane Lenssen, Gene Peach, Lucy Collier, Suzanne Wallis, Marie Markesteyn, Richard Sims, Lisa Pacheco, Anna Gallegos, Beth Hadas, Patrick Moore, C. J. Law, Travis Law, Roger Hubert, Gilbert Jose Vigil, Katherine Wells, Jacobo de la Serna, Antonio Jose "Galento" Martinez, Edward Crocker, Tomas Jaehn, Rowena Mills, Thomas Noeding, Elizabeth Ehrnst, Tori Duggan, and MacKenzie Salisbury.

Foreword

PATRICK MOORE

MICHAEL WALLIS DESCRIBES LOS LUCEROS as "a well-kept secret—a treasure waiting to be rediscovered." Today, the nearly 150 acres that make up the Los Luceros Historic Property in Alcalde, New Mexico, just north of Española off US 68 on the banks of the Río Grande, where ancient peoples once farmed and dwelled, are located next to two vibrant Pueblo communities. Los Luceros stands as the final remnants of the original fifty-thousand-acre Sebastián Martín Serrano Spanish land grant. With a legacy that encompasses centuries of overlapping cultural histories, the property is not just a New Mexican treasure but a national gem.

Wallis masterfully weaves the story of Los Luceros throughout the larger context of northern New Mexico history, from the earliest human inhabitants to the present day, rightly casting it as a pivotal part of Southwest heritage. Recognizing the nuances of contested space, he does not shy away from the complicated overlapping histories of indigenous people, Spanish colonists, and westward United States expansion, all set within the context of water rights and associated power. His thoughtful approach provides a foundation for future understanding.

Today, Los Luceros is reclaiming its traditional place among the communities of northern New Mexico, hosting harvest festivals, showcasing agricultural traditions, holding community celebrations, interpreting the history of northern New Mexico and the terminus of El Camino Real de Tierra Adentro, and more.

Visitors walking along the Río Grande

When former New Mexico Historic Sites director Richard Sims embarked upon this project with author Michael Wallis and photographer Gene Peach, with the support of John Lenssen, they were indeed taking a critical step toward preserving this cultural treasure. These efforts rekindled an awareness of the historic significance of the site. The New Mexico Department of Cultural Affairs and New Mexico Historic Sites are actively working with Los Amigos del Rancho Los Luceros, community groups, farmers, ranchers, Río Arriba and Santa Fe County extension offices, the New Mexico Acequia Association, the Pajarito Environmental Education Center, and other partners to share Los Luceros with visitors and chart the best possible path forward for the historic property.

Los Luceros is an important piece of our shared history and remains a part of all New Mexicans. This book provides a key to understanding that history, and I hope that whatever the future holds for Los Luceros, it will remain a treasure for future generations.

Los Luceros

1 First There Was the Land

Flanked by mountains and mesas and cradled in a bend of the Río Grande in the Española Valley of north-central New Mexico is Los Luceros. The core of an early Spanish land grant, this site has been known by various names over many centuries. The one that stuck is Los Luceros—The Morning Stars.

Just a few miles northeast of the city of Española and the Tewa-speaking Indian pueblo of Ohkay Owingeh (for many years known as San Juan Pueblo), Los Luceros remains a long way from anywhere. In spite of its proximity to Santa Fe, only twenty-five miles to the south, most New Mexicans have never heard of Los Luceros, let alone paid a visit. It is a well-kept secret—a treasure waiting to be rediscovered.

Los Luceros has had a multitude of owners, but in truth, it cannot be possessed. Instead, it needs to be cared for and managed. That has happened at times in the past, and it can happen again. It must happen again. This place with all it represents has to be protected, preserved, and made available to the public.

A mélange of cultures converged here: Tewa, Spanish, Anglo, and the mixed-blood descendants of all of them. Traces remain of the celebrated and the nameless, the famous and the infamous, the *patrones* (landlords), and those who worked in the fields and orchards.

The list of luminaries who spent time at Los Luceros is as varied as it is impressive. It includes Tewa chieftains, caciques, and spiritual leaders; Spanish grandees and conquistadores; a host of traders, soldiers, scouts, and political leaders; and all stripes of artists, writers, and motion-picture stars. Nathan Boone, son of

Full moonrise over upper Río Grande valley

Unknown photographer. *Road to Los Luceros from main highway,* undated.
Maria Chabot Papers, 1866-2002, undated. Georgia O'Keeffe Museum.
Gift of Maria Chabot [2013.3.3].

legendary trailblazer Daniel Boone, camped at Los Luceros with his dragoons
during the Mexican War. Georgia O'Keeffe was a frequent guest, as were Mabel
Dodge Luhan and many from her renowned entourage, including D. H. Lawrence
and Thornton Wilder.

During Mary Cabot Wheelwright's long reign at Los Luceros, at a party in
the magnificent entertainment hall, or sala, of the Casa Grande, the young Leon-
ard Bernstein mesmerized guests for hours playing the grand piano that John D.
Rockefeller Jr. had presented to Wheelwright as a hostess gift. Muhammad Ali and
the acclaimed dancer Gregory Hines came for a day and enjoyed a lunch of fancy
sandwiches at the River House perched on the east bank of the Río Grande.
Robert Redford came close to turning the 148-acre property into an outpost of
creativity for Native Americans and Hispanics interested in filmmaking, the arts,
and the environment. Regrettably, that plan, like many others, was derailed.

Nevertheless, Los Luceros endures. Like the ghosts and specters from long ago, tales of high jinks and intrigue abound. The best ones are true, handed down through the generations like cherished heirlooms.

Whether they only paused for a bit of comfort while passing by, stayed as guests, or lived, worked, and died there, it is apparent that many people have felt a sense of place at Los Luceros. Myths were created and history was made on this land. Traditions, rituals, customs, and heritage survive at Los Luceros and have blended into a rich and potent concoction that nourishes and keeps alive a legacy essential to the identity of New Mexico and its people.

Author Wallace Stegner suggested that our country needs to have a different attitude toward the land, a "sense not of ownership but of belonging." To acquire that sense and appreciate all that Los Luceros represents, it is important to go back to the long-ago past.

Go back before there was the linear oasis known as the *bosque*, Spanish for "woods," the forest of great cottonwoods bordering both sides of the Río Grande. Go back before the impressive mesa of volcanic rock was molded across the river from Los Luceros. Go back before the arrival of the first tribal people who tattooed the black basalt rock faces of the mesa with images and symbols.

Go back and imagine. Imagine what Los Luceros must have been like long ago, a century ago, a millennium ago, or still longer. Envision the land when there was no one to keep time. There was light and darkness, and there were shades of gray. Forged by molten lava and meteor showers and scoured by ice, the land replaced a warm, shallow equatorial sea. Picture the bones of the land being formed and what it was like when granite mountains rose and volcanoes fell asleep and glaciers that sculpted the landscape vanished. Creatures appeared and disappeared—long-necked dinosaurs, flying reptiles with fifty-foot wingspans, ferocious dog-sized lizards, ancestors of horses, giant ground sloths, mastodons, and other prehistoric animals. All of them—the hunters and the hunted and all the rest that followed—were nameless. So were the rivers, mountains, canyons, and mesas. There was no one to name them. There were no cities, villages, or pueblos. There were no soldiers, no warriors, no priests, no shamans, no missionaries, and no bureaucrats or politicians. It was eons before there were Indian boarding schools, prisons, shopping malls, highways, ski lodges, and casinos. There were no churches, temples, or kivas because there was no one to conceive of any god.

Then humans came, and the land was never quite the same.

Previous spread: Freezing mist rises from the Río Grande at dawn in early March

Above: Los Luceros wildlife: bald eagle, sandhill cranes, great blue heron, redtail hawk

Opposite: Irrigation channel in bosque at dawn

Following spread: View of Barranca Mesa and the Jemez Mountains from Los Luceros

2   Tewa Homeland

One is not born a Tewa but rather one is made a Tewa. . . .
Once made, one has to work hard continuously throughout one's life
to remain a Tewa.

—ALFONSO ORTIZ (OHKAY OWINGEH PUEBLO), *THE TEWA WORLD*

THE HUMAN HISTORY OF WHAT IS NOW LOS LUCEROS began long before the Spanish
set foot in the Americas. Distinct tribal cultures emerged from the first inhabitants of
New Mexico, including a group of hunters and gatherers who built homes beneath
overhanging cliffs, crafted pottery and baskets, and learned how to live in harmony
with the land, the rivers, the elements, and the heavens. Some of those people were
linguistically connected by a branch of the Tanoan language family called Tewa.

According to Tewa history, their ancestors came from a place to the north,
beneath a lake in present-day Colorado. In this underworld, humans and animals
lived together, along with supernatural beings, and death was unknown. The sun
shone only at night, as pale as the moon. After climbing a great fir tree, the Tewa
emerged into the world and migrated south.

Over time, they eventually made settlements on both sides of the Río Grande
and the Chama River. By AD 1200, these Puebloans were ensconced in the upper
Río Grande valley, where their ancestors had hunted and gathered food for thousands of years.

When the Spanish arrived a few centuries later, they called the villages—
clusters of adobe dwellings around a central plaza—*pueblos*, the Spanish word for

Mesa Prieta petroglyphs

"town" or "village." Along or near P'osonghe, the Tewa name of the Río Grande, some of those pueblos—Ohkay Owingeh, Santa Clara, San Ildefonso, Nambé, and Pojoaque—remain.

Ohkay Owingeh is the home of descendants of the first people known to have lived on the nearby land now called Los Luceros. That ancestral pueblo of Ohkay Owingeh was built on a grassy plain, or *llano*, overlooking from the east the Los Luceros of today, making it one of the oldest continuously inhabited sites on the North American continent. It was called Pioge (sometimes spelled Phioge), the Place of the Woodpeckers. Woodpeckers and their flicker cousins still thrive at Los Luceros.

Tewa people dwelled at Pioge as early as AD 1200, before the Río Grande shifted its course to the west, and occupied it to at least AD 1550, if not longer. Pioge was one of the larger settlements, with five room blocks built of puddled adobe around a central plaza and smaller pueblos and field houses on the property of today's Los Luceros.

Like so many other ancestral pueblos, Pioge no longer stands. Through the years, a combination of the elements, historic land use, construction, and cultivation obscured the site. Still, bits and pieces of the past remain in the soil of Los Luceros. Archaeologists have found thousands of artifacts. Potsherds, including examples of pottery that had been fired but not glazed, washed down from the Pioge site into the orchards and fields. They serve as a form of memory and furnish evidence of the past. These discoveries help to remind us that long before the Spanish came to this land, the early Tewas enjoyed a settled way of life.

They tended terraced gardens bordered by smooth rock cobbles from the nearby river and irrigated with seasonal runoff. They planted and harvested corn, beans, squash, and other staples. In addition to practicing agriculture, they hunted deer, turkey, and other game in the bosque and fished in the big river and its tributaries. They engineered roads, made pilgrimages to the shrines of their ancestors, and enacted age-old religious beliefs and sacred ceremonies. They studied the heavens. The stars, the sun, and the moon regulated Tewa lives.

Clans and societies were tied to the seasons and the solstices. The people welcomed the rain and snow showers and the spring wind that flushed out the last of winter. They closely followed the travels of the sun and moon. Rainbows, comets, clouds, thunder, and lightning had special meanings. The Tewas watched the first silent stars of evening and the flow of the Milky Way, 'Opatuk'u (Backbone of the Universe).

All celestial bodies had a place in tribal customs and rituals. The Tewas carved alabaster fetishes and painted images of rain clouds, water snakes, and dragonflies and sacred symbols on pottery. Like their ancestors, the Tewas meticulously etched tens of thousands of petroglyphs into the massive basalt boulders on the west side of the Río Grande that came to be known as Mesa Prieta (Black Mesa), often called Mesa de La Canoa (Canoe Mesa) because of its oblong shape.

"To us, these petroglyphs are not the remnants of some long lost civilization that has been dead for many years. . . . They are part of our living culture," said Herman Agoyo, former governor of Ohkay Owingeh Pueblo, quoted by Michael Hartranft in the *Albuquerque Journal*. "What is stored in the petroglyphs is not written in any book or found in any library. We need to return to them to remind us of who we are and where we came from, and to teach our own sons and daughters of it."

The Tewas of Pioge found spiritual meaning in the basalt cliffs, the distant mountain peaks, the big river, and the earth itself. The same was true at the other pueblos of the Tewa homeland, whose population more than doubled in the late thirteenth and early fourteenth centuries as a pronounced increase in migration was sparked in part by climate change. A lengthy period of extreme winter weather that impacted much of the planet from about 1300 to 1750 came to be known as the Little Ice Age. Extreme drought and disease also took a toll, forcing people to seek more healthful climates.

By the mid-1500s, many people from Pioge as well as the ancestral pueblos of Sajiu-uingge and Pojiu-uningge had moved just a few miles south to another Tewa community on the east bank of the Río Grande just north of the confluence with the Chama River. It was Ohkay Owingeh, or the Place of the Strong People. According to some sources, the Tewas knew the large pueblo simply as Oke, sometimes spelled Okeh or Ohke. An earlier Oke Pueblo about a mile to the north had been swept away in a flood. According to tribal lore, the flood was caused when a Tewa man in seclusion during a twelve-day ceremonial fast became so crazed for water that he broke out of the chamber where he was confined. He rushed to the bosque and drank so much river water that he burst open and the water from his body washed over the pueblo and left it in ruins.

A second pueblo named Oke was built in the same lowlands but was later abandoned, and the tribe moved to higher ground and built the pueblo that stands today. Directly across from Oke, on the east side of the Río Grande, was still another pueblo. It was named Yungue-Ouinge, meaning Mockingbird Place.

Abandoning crowded or declining villages to be absorbed into the population of another pueblo was always a viable option. Migration—even if only a short distance—was intrinsic in Tewa culture, a fundamental part of their origin story.

Deer Dance at Ohkay Owingeh Pueblo

Movement is one of the ideological concepts of Pueblo thought because
it is necessary for the perpetuation of life. Movement, clouds, wind, and
rain are one. Movement must be emulated by the people. Movement is
part of us. . . . Without movement, there is no life.

—TESSIE NARANJO (SANTA CLARA PUEBLO), TEWA SCHOLAR

As essential as movement was to the Tewas, their relationship with the land was
just as important. Property ownership was unknown to them, as it was to most
tribal people. They lived communally and made no claims on their surroundings.
Instead of a desire to possess the land, they had a sense of belonging to their place.

In the waning years of the sixteenth century, the Tewa way of life was about
to change dramatically. A new tribe unlike any other people the Pueblos had
ever seen would soon arrive. They came astride snorting beasts with long manes
that some Pueblo people called the Great Dogs of the White Men. The men had
beards and spoke a strange tongue. Some of them wore helmets and chain mail
or quilted cotton body armor. Some had steel lances and swords. Others carried
matchlock muskets or crossbows.

They did not come to visit. They came to stay. They came to capture Tewa
souls and own the land.

3   La Entrada

THE ENTRY OF THE SPANISH INTO THE TEWA HOMELAND was inevitable as early as 1519, after conquistador Hernán Cortés and his army arrived in present-day Mexico hundreds of miles to the south. In a little more than two years, the Aztecs were vanquished and their empire's culture virtually destroyed. Before long, tantalizing rumors drew the victorious Spaniards to the great cities of gold said to be located in the far northern reaches of Nueva España.

In 1540, Francisco Vázquez de Coronado, chasing a dream of wealth, commanded the first officially authorized expedition to the mysterious land in the north. This was the first Spanish expedition known to have reached the site of Los Luceros—at the time, raw and open land—and the nearby Tewa Pueblos.

In July 1541, one of Coronado's senior officers, Captain Francisco de Barrionuevo, and some of his troops were dispatched on an exploratory trip up the Río Grande to gather fresh provisions. The foraging party entered the valley of the Tewas and paused at several pueblos, including one that the Spanish later named San Ildefonso. When they came upon Ohkay Owingeh and Yungue-Ouinge on the opposite side of the river, the soldiers found both pueblos deserted. Apparently, the villagers had been forewarned of the approaching strangers and had left to hide in other pueblos.

"At Yuqueyunque [Yungue-Ouinge] the whole nation left two very fine villages which they had on the other side of the river entirely vacant, and went

31

into the mountains, where they had four very strong villages in a rough country, where it was impossible for horses to go," Pedro de Castañeda, the chronicler of the Coronado expedition, recorded in his journal. "In the two villages there was a great deal of food and some very beautiful glazed earthenware with many figures and different shapes. Here they also found many bowls full of a carefully selected shining metal with which they glazed the earthenware. This shows that mines of silver would be found in that country if they should hunt for them."

Coronado's exhausting two-year exploratory trek yielded neither silver nor gold. What he and his cohorts found was a highly organized civilization made up of villages that were fiercely independent and that operated autonomously, with no central authority. After a near-fatal tumble from his horse, a disappointed Coronado and his weary troops headed back to Mexico, where further interest in exploring the northern frontier quickly waned.

No further attempts were made to explore today's New Mexico for forty years. In 1581, some zealous Franciscan friars, eager to save pagan souls, journeyed there but were killed by Pueblo people with bitter memories of the harsh treatment meted out by Coronado's soldiers. The following year, a party of Spanish colonists trekked north but lasted only a few months before fear and internal dissent ended their mission.

Back in Spain, there was a growing financial crisis. The turning point came in 1588, when the English Royal Navy decimated the mighty Spanish Armada. This fiasco shattered both Spain's morale and its failing economy. King Phillip II, waging wars on three fronts, also had to pay royal guards and maintain frontier garrisons. He needed to pay for the recently completed construction of El Escorial, a palatial royal palace and monastery complex. Any spare money went toward the monumental royal debt. For years, Spain took in a steady flow of precious metal that was mined, melted down, and minted in South America and Nueva España. In some places, the mines were playing out. New territory needed to be explored, especially the vast lands to the north.

In 1590, Gaspar Castaño de Sosa, a Portuguese native, led an unauthorized expedition from Nueva España into "la nueva México." Hopeful of establishing his own colony, he brought a large number of prospective settlers and herds of livestock, but unlike other expeditions, not one Catholic priest. Castaño de Sosa was credited with coming up with the name Río Grande when the illegal party crossed the river. They followed the stream to the Pecos River and continued on to Pecos Pueblo, where they briefly skirmished with the residents. In the winter of

1591, the company moved north to the heartland of Pueblo country. They stopped at Pioge, Ohkay Owingeh, and Yungue-Ouinge but quickly moved on to other pueblos.

After wandering among scores of pueblos along the Río Grande, Castaño de Sosa's hope of building his own fiefdom ended. There were no caches of mineral wealth, and his followers were considering mutiny when a troop of soldiers dispatched by Spanish authorities caught up with the company. Castaño de Sosa was taken back to Mexico City in irons. In 1593, he was tried and convicted for his illegal invasion of lands inhabited by peaceful Indians and for other crimes and was sentenced to six years of exile in the Philippines. His sentence was appealed to the Council of the Indies and eventually reversed, but by then, Castaño de Sosa had been killed by Chinese slaves during a ship mutiny near the Molucca Islands. However, his dream of conquering and colonizing the frontier north of Nueva España was still alive.

The people of the pueblos remained on alert even after the many failed attempts by the Spanish to take control of the Tewa homeland. They had looked into the eyes of the soldiers and priests and could see their resolve. They knew that more white men would come bearing both the sword and the cross.

That day came on April 30, 1598, on the banks of the Río Grande just south of where the city of El Paso, Texas, was later founded. Don Juan de Oñate took possession of all of New Mexico in the name of the "Most Holy Trinity" and King Phillip II, just months before the monarch died.

In his new role as "governor and captain general, and Adelantado of New Mexico, and all its kingdoms and provinces," Oñate performed a formal ceremony to claim the new land. The official proclamation that he read to his company of soldiers, colonists, slaves, and priests clearly stated that Spain now had dominion over literally everything and everyone in the region.

Oñate scrawled his name and titles on the document in the presence of the throng of witnesses from his command as well as the royal notary. That single act on the river's edge laid the foundation for more than two centuries of Spanish rule in the Southwest. It gave Oñate the legal authority to conquer and colonize the entire province.

The date also happened to be the Feast of the Ascension, the Catholic commemoration of the bodily ascension of Jesus Christ into heaven. A bower was made from mesquite branches, and the Franciscan priests said a mass of thanksgiving. "We built a great bonfire and roasted meat and fish, and then sat down to a repast the like of which we had never enjoyed before," wrote Gaspar Pérez de Villagrá, the official historian of the Oñate expedition.

Much celebration followed. People shouted, muskets were fired into the air, and trumpets blared. There was music and theatrical entertainment. A feast was prepared, and just before it was served, Oñate nailed a small cross to a tree and offered a prayer of thanksgiving.

For the rest of his life, Oñate fondly remembered that April day on the Río Grande, or, as he called it, Río del Norte, the name that it would mostly be known by for the next 250 years. Oñate had been born in New Spain to a prosperous family that controlled silver mines near Zacatecas. He pursued the mining business but also commanded military operations in battles against nomadic tribes who fiercely resisted the encroachment of the Spanish into their territory. The young nobleman gained more riches and prestige through his marriage to Isabel de Tolosa Cortés de Moctezuma, a wealthy mestiza (mixed-blood) mining heiress. She was the granddaughter of Hernán Cortés, the Spanish conqueror of Mexico, and great-granddaughter of the Aztec emperor Moctezuma II.

The couple soon had a son and daughter and enjoyed a comfortable life. Oñate, however, grew restless. When he learned that another exploratory expedition to the far north was being planned, he was ecstatic. He longed for a challenge. After years of pursuing a military career and prospecting for silver, Oñate, hungry for more fame and fortune, jumped at the opportunity to lead the Spanish Crown's colonizing venture into northern New Spain.

There was fierce competition, but Oñate was well liked by many people in positions of influence and power. Among them was his political patron, Luís de Velasco, who, as viceroy of New Spain, was in charge of appointing the expedition leader. It came as no surprise when Oñate was awarded the command in 1595. But before the agreement could be executed, a newly appointed viceroy put the expedition on hold while he reviewed the paperwork. The bureaucratic delay caused some of the colonists who had been recruited for the expedition to change their minds. At last, on January 26, 1598, after waiting almost two-and-a-half years, the expeditionary force was permitted to leave for New Mexico.

Oñate's caravan stretched for several miles. It comprised an estimated five hundred men, women, and children, including mestizos, the result of Spanish and Indian intermarriage, conversos, Jews who had converted to Catholicism to avoid the Holy Office of the Inquisition, and Crypto-Jews, who had concealed their Jewish identity. Along with the families were soldiers, Franciscan friars, servants, and Indian, mulatto, and mestizo slaves. Depending on social standing, they rode horseback or walked. Some found places in wagons and carretas, huge two-wheeled carts pulled by oxen and loaded with tools, household items, armaments, food supplies, trade goods, and worldly possessions.

Astride a prancing charger, Oñate led his intrepid company up El Camino Real Tierra Adentro, the Royal Road of the Interior Land, an ancient path used by many Indian people for hundreds of years as a communications and trade route.

The journey north was not easy. Cattle went astray, the desert was excruciatingly hot by day and cold at night, and potable water was difficult to find. After putting up with fifty days of hardship and suffering, more than a few of the colonists were beginning to have second thoughts. When the weary band first spied the waters of the Río Grande, there was great joy. It was April 30, 1598.

After a celebration, the expedition moved on to the present site of El Paso, Texas, and crossed to the other side of the river. The long procession continued northward into the upper Río Grande valley, traversing some of the countryside that Coronado had explored decades earlier.

The travelers briefly stopped at several Native settlements, including Kewa, the largest pueblo in New Mexico, which Oñate called Santo Domingo because the colonists arrived on a Sunday. He persuaded the reluctant Pueblo leaders to gather in a kiva to render their allegiance to Phillip II of Spain and to the Pope and then kneel and kiss the ring of a friar. Oñate and his band then pushed on.

Just north of Santo Domingo, where the Río Grande enters a long, impassable canyon, one of many on this stretch, the Spaniards detoured and scaled La Bajada (The Descent), a steep volcanic mesa. From that point, at the summit of the cliff of black basalt, the Oñate party left what is known as the Río Abajo (Lower River) and continued into the more mountainous Río Arriba (Upper River) to the north.

By July 1598, Oñate and some of his soldiers reached the Tewa-speaking villages on the east bank of the Río Grande, near what became Los Luceros. Oñate immediately took control of Ohkay Owingeh. All the inhabitants gathered and swore loyalty to the Spanish Crown. As royal vassals, they now served as a labor force and provided their conquerors with food and other necessities. The camp was renamed San Juan de los Caballeros, or St. John of the Warrior Knights, in honor of John the Baptist and in tribute to the Spanish newcomers.

Soon swarms of rodents and insects appeared, and living conditions in the overcrowded village became increasingly uncomfortable. Oñate decided to move. The colony relocated just across the Río Grande and took over the Tewa Pueblo of Yunque-Ouinge. The colonists persuaded the occupants to leave their homes and move to San Juan. Soon the Spanish built a church and transformed the pueblo into a village they renamed San Gabriel del Yunque—the sole Spanish settlement in the colony and the first capital of New Mexico.

With San Gabriel as a base, Governor Oñate and his forces set out to complete the establishment of the Spanish Empire in New Mexico. They surveyed the pueblos up and down the Río Grande and scouted the outlying countryside, mountains, and plains in search of mineral riches. Far to the west, at the ancient Acoma Pueblo, a natural citadel on a sandstone mesa jutting 367 feet above the desert floor, a band of Spanish scouts encountered stiff resistance from people unwilling to cave in to the demands of invaders. After the Acomas killed several Spanish soldiers, including one of Oñate's nephews, the governor and his officers decided to teach them a lesson.

In due course, Oñate dispatched a force of well-armed soldiers eager to exact revenge. The fighting on both sides was fierce, but the courageous inhabitants of Acoma could not withstand the cannon fire and deadly assault. Hundreds of them perished in the devastation. The victorious Spaniards plundered and burned the houses and made hundreds of men, women, and children prisoners. Then they escorted the subdued Acoma defenders to Santo Domingo Pueblo for trial.

The resulting punishment was severe for all the culprits, including twenty-four men over the age of twenty-five. Oñate determined their punishment would be "to have one foot cut off and twenty years of personal servitude." The other unfortunate captives avoided mutilation but ended up condemned to years of slavery and service to their Spanish overlords. Such cruel measures, along with repeated attempts to decimate Pueblo culture, did little to endear the interlopers to the original New Mexicans.

Meanwhile, back in the Río Arriba, the fledgling capital of San Gabriel was struggling, despite the infusion of fresh settlers. Harsh winter storms, mutinies caused by dissent over Oñate's leadership, and severe food shortages took a heavy toll.

After several more grueling years and a barrage of complaints from the colonists, Oñate fell out of favor with almost everyone. By 1607, he had resigned the governorship of New Mexico. He remained with the colony at San Gabriel for a time before royal authorities recalled him to Mexico. Forever banished from New Mexico, the discredited nobleman ultimately stood trial. Absolved of some crimes, he was convicted on a variety of other charges, mostly stemming from his mismanagement of the colony and abuse of Pueblo people. Stripped of all titles and heavily fined, Oñate moved to Spain, where he finally cleared his name, saw his titles restored, and served as royal inspector of mines until his death in 1627.

By then, Oñate's original colony in New Mexico was long gone from San Gabriel on the banks of the Río Grande. Don Pedro de Peralta, the new royal governor, moved most of the colonists south from the river and the heavy concentration of Tewa Pueblos. Peralta and his followers settled at the site of an abandoned Indian ruin, strategically situated at the southern end of the Sangre de Cristo Mountains. The newly founded La Villa Real de la Santa Fé de San Francisco de Asís, which translates to The Royal City of the Holy Faith of Saint Francis of Assisi, became the capital of the province.

San Gabriel did not vanish overnight, however. Even after the seat of government shifted to Santa Fe, some Spanish colonists chose to remain in the area. Documents dated as late as 1617 make reference to San Gabriel. Then the old pueblo was largely forgotten for two hundred years.

In the late 1890s, the site was rediscovered, but not much preservation or investigation occurred until the 1940s, when a team of archaeologists excavated

University of New Mexico excavation of San Gabriel del Yunque Ouinge in northern New Mexico, 1962. Palace of the Governors Photo Archives (NMHM/DCA 042236).

the adobe ruin. There were further explorations in the 1960s. A piece of a bronze bell, the crown of a fifteenth-century archer's helmet, an engraved gunstock, religious medals, and candlesticks provided evidence of those who had once lived there. Eventually, the adobes were removed from exposed walls to be used elsewhere, and in 1984, the remains of San Gabriel were leveled and the land planted in alfalfa. Today there is only a cross and a plaque on a brick memorial.

> JULY 11, 1598, JUAN DE OÑATE,
> COLONIZER, ESTABLISHED THE FIRST
> SPANISH CAPITAL IN THIS PUEBLO.
> THE INDIANS RECEIVED THE SPANIARDS
> WITH GREAT COURTESY. THEREAFTER
> THE PUEBLO WAS KNOWN AS SAN JUAN
> DE LOS CABALLEROS. LATER OÑATE
> MOVED THE CAPITAL INTO LARGER
> QUARTERS AND NAMED IT SAN GABRIEL.
>
> NEW MEXICO STATE SOCIETY
> DAUGHTERS OF THE AMERICAN COLONISTS, 1964

Oñate was not forgotten. He is a divisive figure to this day, regarded by some as New Mexico's founding father and by others as a ruthless conqueror.

The Oñate Monument and Visitors Center officially opened in 1994 on the shoulder of New Mexico State Highway 68, only a short distance from Los Luceros. In front of the building and atop a concrete base, visitors were greeted by a larger-than-life bronze statue of Oñate on horseback. At New Year's 1998—the four-hundredth anniversary of the first permanent European settlement in the American West—unknown persons, described by James Brooke in *The New York Times* as an "Indian commando group," used an electric saw to sever the statue's booted right foot. "We took the liberty of removing Oñate's right foot on behalf of brothers and sisters of Acoma Pueblo, read a released statement. "We see no glory in celebrating Oñate's fourth centennial, and we do not want our faces rubbed in it."

A new foot was cast and attached to the statue at taxpayers' cost. The visitor center never got off the ground. It closed, and tenants came and went, including a Montessori school, a flea market, and a yoga studio. The statue of Don Juan de Oñate is still there. His cold eyes are locked in a perpetual stare beyond the highway traffic at the land and the dark mesa where there are signs and symbols of long ago that he never understood.

A cross and memorial at San Gabriel del Yunque-Ouinge,
a National Historic Landmark

4   La Soledad

IN THE EARLY YEARS OF THE SEVENTEENTH CENTURY when San Gabriel was still standing, the Los Luceros property that exists today began to emerge.

Archaeological evidence suggests that soon after the arrival of the first wave of Spanish colonists, the future Los Luceros was the site of a defensive outpost to protect against intruders. Part of that adobe outpost might have been incorporated into the construction of the original Casa Grande, which over time evolved into the magnificent adobe hacienda that remains as a symbol of the once grand estate.

During the 1600s, the land seems to have been periodically used for agriculture and ranching. Historians conjecture that a member of the Lucero de Godoy family built a small four-room adobe on the property. If true, that would have been prior to August 10, 1680, the beginning of the Pueblo Revolt, the earliest and most successful Native insurrection along the northern frontier. On that day, the Pueblo people, weary of religious and economic oppression at the hands of their Spanish masters and Franciscan priests, launched a fierce offensive that drove the interlopers out of New Mexico.

Popé (sometimes spelled Popay), a Tewa religious leader from Ohkay Owingeh who lived at Taos, galvanized the northern pueblos in the united rebellion. The countryside quickly exploded into a bloody revolt. Most of the northern settlers and Franciscans in the outlying areas were massacred. Many of the colonists and mestizos in the Río Arriba escaped to Santa Fe and took shelter in the Palace of the Governors, but angry Pueblo people, determined to end Spanish domination and exploitation, stormed the capital city. Survivors retreated southward on El Camino Real along with other refugees from the Río Abajo to present El Paso.

For the next twelve years, the colony ceased to exist, and the old San Gabriel settlement and nearby ranchos bordering the Río Grande remained abandoned. That changed in 1692 when the newly appointed governor and captain-general of New Mexico, Don Diego de Vargas Zapata y Luján Ponce de Léon y Contreras, led his army from El Paso along the Río Grande to Santa Fe.

A nobleman with two decades of experience as a warrior in New Spain, Don Diego de Vargas was determined to retake the province from Indian insurgents. He quickly found that as he pushed northward, most of the Pueblo Indian alliance had collapsed. Even so, it was not a completely bloodless reconquest. Over the course of several years spent in crushing the Pueblo rebels, Vargas ordered the public executions of scores of captives and sentenced hundreds more to long terms as slaves. Spanish military forces encountered determined opposition and resistance to the recolonization until 1696.

At the same time, many of the colonists who had fled the province a dozen years before returned to rebuild and carve out places for themselves on the northern frontier. There would never be another major rebellion of the Pueblos under Spanish rule. Weary of war, the colonists slowly began to compromise. Both sides made an effort to diminish tensions and strive for peaceful coexistence to provide a common defense against the relentless raids of Utes, Comanches, Navajos, and Apaches on Spanish settlements and the pueblos of the Río Arriba.

The new century brought the promise of change and fresh beginnings. The reconquest by Vargas opened the land and stimulated settlement. One of many parties interested in a fresh beginning was Sebastián Martín Serrano, a strong political leader, fierce war captain, and veteran of the Vargas force that took back the province during the reconquest. In 1703, the earliest written record of settlement on the Los Luceros property appeared in a land grant made to Capitán Martín, as his friends and associates called him. (Serrano was dropped from the family surname in the 1700s.)

Martín and his wife, María Luján, whose family had been massacred at Taos during the 1680 Pueblo Revolt, resided in reoccupied Santa Fe until 1698. Then they returned north to the Río Arriba, where Martín's parents and grandparents had lived before the uprising. After settling at La Villa Nueva de Santa Cruz de la Cañada, he and his brother Antonio set out to acquire a sizable tract of land for themselves, their other brothers and a brother-in-law, Felipe Antonio Cisneros, who was married to Josefa Luján, the sister of Sebastian's wife, Maria Luján.

The search took them north of Ohkay Owingeh on the Río Grande, where they found a large tract of land that looked promising. They proceeded to Santa Fe to petition for a land grant from Governor Vargas only to find that sometime in the past, the land had been granted to a consortium that included Joseph Chacón Medina, Sebastián de Polonia, Sebastián de Vargas, and others. The Martín brothers pointed out that the land was not occupied, as required by Spanish law. Vargas looked into the matter and verified that the land had indeed been abandoned. He declared that the original claimants had forfeited their rights and immediately granted the land to the Martíns. Vargas also issued an order forbidding the original owners ever to lay claim to the land.

The Martíns moved to what Sebastián Martín described as "a vacant, uncultivated, and unoccupied tract of land in Río Arriba, a short distance from the pueblo of San Juan," according to architectural historian Betsy Swanson's nomination of Los Luceros to the National Register of Historic Places. The abandoned ruins of Pioge served as a temporary residence while they rebuilt a nearby ramshackle adobe house. It might have been the remains of a four-room building that had been owned by Juan de Dios Lucero de Godoy or a member of his family before the 1680 rebellion.

Over the next few years, Martín and his brothers made other improvements and cleared the fields for cultivation. In 1706, raiding Apaches killed Antonio Sisneros, Sebastián Martín's brother-in-law and partner. The following year, Martín bought out the widow, his wife's sister, for 150 pesos and, as a goodwill gesture, presented her three orphaned children with "a little Indian of six or seven years of age, a cow and a young ox." He also allowed the family to continue to reside on the land, although several years later, the Sisneros heirs took Martín to court and won back a portion of the grant so that they could build a larger home and plant grain crops.

In 1712, Martín bought out his brother Antonio's interest in the grant but lost the deed. To confirm his ownership, Martín petitioned Governor José Chacón Medina Salazar y Villaseñor. According to Ralph Emerson Twitchell, Sebastian Martín testified that he and his brothers had "broken up lands, opened a main ditch from the Río Norte for irrigating the land, built a house with four rooms, and two strong towers for defense against the enemy in case of an invasion, being on the frontier." The governor decided for Martín and validated his ownership.

The Sebastián Martín land grant covered more than fifty thousand acres. It extended five miles upriver, from San Juan Pueblo on the south to Picuris Pueblo on the north. It also stretched for eighteen miles, from Mesa Prieta to the forested

William Henry Jackson, *Principal irrigating canal at the Pueblo of San Juan,*
ca. 1880s. Palace of the Governors Photo Archives (NMHM/DCA 049167).

peaks of the Sangre de Cristos on the east. In 1751, Martín gave a portion of the
land close to the mountains to twelve colonists so that they could establish the village of Las Trampas.

Despite an assortment of difficulties and dangers—the constant threat of
Plains Indian attacks, epidemics, drought, floods, and other acts of God and man—
Martín and his family made good use of the land grant in the bottomlands north
of San Juan. Martín gave the people at San Juan Pueblo a parcel of valley land in
exchange for their help in digging the first acequia on the east side of the Río
Grande. Known as Sebastián Martín's ditch, that acequia still serves Los Luceros.
On the irrigated plowed property, Martín planted hundreds of apple trees, a large
cornfield, and a garden of chile and onions. On the rest of the land, he grazed
cattle, horses, and sheep. He named the settlement Puesto de Nuestra Señora de la
Soledad del Río del Norte Arriba, Outpost of Our Lady of Solitude of the Upper
River of the North. Most of the frontier settlers called it La Soledad, a fitting title
for the lonely retreat just south of the fertile fields of today's Los Luceros.

From 1747 until 1750, an increase in Ute Indian raids caused the residents to
abandon La Soledad and other northern settlements. Once the authorities had
restored peace and posted guards for protection, the citizens returned to their

homes and farms. Captain Martín built an adobe house with a pair of round towers, or torreones, to defend against raids by Comanches or Apaches. Over the years, as Martín and his wife raised ten children, several of whom they survived, the house increased from four rooms to twenty-four, along with a stable and storage area, all under one flat mud roof supported by huge vigas. Besides all the family members, the house also accommodated animals and at least twenty-one household servants, mostly Navajo, Ute, Apache, and Comanche slaves.

Martín died in 1763 at the age of ninety-two. The frontier outpost of forty-four families totaled 364 people, according to a 1750 census report, and grew larger when Martín's widow died and her last will and testament became public in 1765. In 1772, the division of La Soledad among the heirs was under way, and within a few more years, maps sometimes referred to the settlement as Río Arriba.

Río Arriba was the name used by Fray Francisco Atanasio Domínguez when he inspected all the Franciscan missions during his tour of New Mexico in 1776. Known to be a harsh critic, Domínguez wrote a tempered description of the chapel built by the Martíns.

William Henry Jackson, *Mission church, San Juan Pueblo, New Mexico,* ca. 1881–1882. Palace of the Governors Photo Archives (NMHM/DCA 043337).

Río Arriba is a league [three miles] north of the mission [at San Juan Pueblo] and up on the same plain. It consists of a number of ranchos. . . . In this little place there is a chapel of Our Lady of Solitude. Its patron was one Sebastián Martín. Today his substitute and heir is a son of his called Marcial Martín. This little chapel is adobe and resembles a small bodega. It faces west and is 14 to 16 varas [one vara is 3½ inches] long, 5 wide, and 6 high. There is no choir loft. There is a poor window in the Epistle side facing south, and the door is squared with one leaf and a key. The roof is wrought beams; there is a small belfry with its brass mortar [bell], and a little cemetery. The only functions here are two novenas and a Mass annually. The alms for this are collected from all the settlers in the mission's district.

—FRAY FRANCISCO ATANASIO DOMÍNGUEZ, IN *THE MISSIONS OF NEW MEXICO, 1776* BY ELEANOR B. ADAMS AND FRAY ANGÉLICO CHÁVEZ

The site of Martín's La Soledad was always the subject of debate. The rancho has been associated with different locales, all near Los Luceros, such as the small communities of Plaza de Alcalde and La Villita.

"Eventually the names Soledad and Río Arriba (referring to a community) fell into disuse, and the exact location of Sebastián Martín's frontier outpost is not precisely known," contends Dr. Corrine P. Sze in a report commissioned in the late 1990s titled *History of the Los Luceros Ranch*.

It is understandable that Sebastián Martín Serrano's large complex with its large, multi-room home, towers, and nearby chapel so precisely described by Domínguez in 1776 has been identified with the most impressive historic building in the area today, the main house of the Los Luceros Ranch. However, a careful examination of available evidence indicates that Soledad, while reduced in importance, survived into the mid-nineteenth century as one among a number of small, closely related river communities, including Los Luceros, which were located on the Sebastián Martín Serrano Grant. . . . As to actual location, there is some indication that Soledad was closer to San Juan than Los Luceros Ranch is today.

Although there is no conclusive evidence, other credible sources have made the case that the site of Casa Grande at Los Luceros might be the location of Sebastián Martín's residence. That argument was made in 1983 when Los Luceros was placed on the National Register of Historic Places.

Matachines Dance at Ohkay Owingeh Pueblo on Christmas Eve

5   Plaza de Los Luceros

By the late 1700s, various Martín family heirs had begun to buy and sell their shares of the property. The trend started soon after Bárbara Padilla, the daughter of Margarita Martín and Juan Antonio Padilla and a granddaughter of Capítan Martín, accepted a proposal of marriage. She wed Santiago Lucero, a descendant of the illustrious Lucero de Godoy family that had helped to colonize New Mexico and might have made an unsuccessful claim on the land grant long controlled by the Martín family. Two founding families of northern New Mexico were thus linked in marriage. Change was imminent.

For a brief time, La Soledad became Plaza de Los Angeles, but by the mid–1800s, that place-name had disappeared. Then finally came the name Plaza de los Luceros or Rancho de Los Luceros or some derivative of Los Luceros, meaning "the Lucero folks" or The Morning Stars.

Title for much of the land grant passed from the Martíns to the Luceros, resulting in progressive subdivision among their joint heirs. For many years, Julián Lucero, nephew of Santiago and Bárbara Lucero, systematically bought parcels of the ranch from the many Martín and Lucero descendants. The abundant harvests from the broad fields and orchards of Los Luceros were consistently profitable. Before 1821 and the opening of the Santa Fe Trail, great herds of sheep from the ranch were being driven eastward to market. By 1827, only six years after Mexico secured its independence from Spain and New Mexico became part of the Mexican nation, Julián Lucero had managed to buy out his siblings and all other heirs to Los Luceros land, including the orchards and much of the outlying property. The enterprising landowner also took a wife. It seems rather fitting that Julián Lucero married Bárbara Antonia Sisneros, a granddaughter of Antonio Sisneros, one of the original partners of the Sebastián Martín land grant many years earlier.

In 1844, when New Mexico was divided into three districts, or *prefecturas*, Los Luceros became the Prefectura del Norte. Long the center of social and political activity in the region, the rancho was now one of three major divisions of the Departamento de Nuevo México. That changed in 1846 when the twenty-five-year period of Mexican rule came to an end with the Mexican-American War. General Stephen Watts Kearny and his Army of the West conquered New Mexico and raised the United States flag over the Palace of the Governors in Santa Fe. According to local lore, during his time in northern New Mexico, Kearny paid a call at Los Luceros and slept behind the thick adobe walls of one of the village homes.

Whether or not the Kearny story is a myth, Los Luceros played an important role in the war. Early on, when news of the coming invasion broke, Colonel José Maria Chávez, from a prominent Abiquiú family, mustered his militia and used the fields of Los Luceros as a training ground. Chávez apparently had the blessing of Julián Lucero and other community landowners and leaders such as Diego Ruperto Archuleta. A true son of the Los Luceros community, Archuleta quickly answered the call when American troops headed down the Santa Fe Trail to take control of the province of New Mexico.

Born at Los Luceros in 1814, Archuleta was a grandson of Santiago Lucero. The boy's parents, Andrés Archuleta and Margarita Antonio Lucero, hoping their son would become a priest, sent him to Durango, México, for his education. After eight years of religious study, Archuleta opted to pursue a military career. In 1840, he graduated from the Heroico Colegio Militar in Mexico City and returned to Los Luceros to be commissioned a captain in the New Mexico militia. When the expansionist-minded Republic of Texas unwisely decided to take a portion of land from New Mexico in 1841, Archuleta was recognized for valor for leading his troops against a force of Texan invaders. He then served as a deputy from New Mexico to the National Mexican Congress.

At the outbreak of the Mexican-American War in 1846, Archuleta was promoted to colonel, second in command of the Mexican forces. He resented the invasion and was determined to fight to his last breath. Unlike General Manuel Armijo, who decided not to take on the Americans and instead fled south to Mexico, Archuleta resisted. He did not waver even after the overthrow of the

Mexican government was completed and Kearny issued a set of new laws that New Mexicans had to follow.

Archuleta would have none of it. He joined with Tomás Ortiz, the former alcalde of Santa Fe and brother of the vicar of Santa Fe, Father Juan Felipe Ortiz, and they came up with a plan to drive the gringos from their land. First, they had to overthrow the newly formed American government headed by Charles Bent, the Taos trader whom Kearny had appointed as governor of the territory. The rebels also had to be aware of the man Kearny had put in charge of maintaining the peace—Colonel Sterling Price, a tobacco planter and politician from Missouri whose regiment of scrappy mounted dragoons lovingly nicknamed him "Old Pap."

Archuleta and Ortiz held clandestine meetings in Santa Fe and at Los Luceros. The insurgents they recruited were a mix of Pueblo and Hispanic people, Catholic priests, and many others from prominent northern New Mexico families. In December 1846, just as the plan was to be carried out, an informant revealed the plot to the Americans.

Pueblo Indians at Los Luceros. Courtesy of Marie Markesteyn.

"About the 15th of December last I received information of an attempt to excite the people of the territory against the American government," Colonel Price wrote in his official report. "This rebellion was headed by Thomas Ortiz and Diego Archuleta. An officer, formerly in the Mexican service, was seized, and on his person was found a list of all the disbanded Mexican soldiers in the vicinity of Santa Fe. Others persons supposed to be implicated were arrested, and a full investigation proved that many of the influential persons in the northern part of this territory were engaged in the rebellion. All attempts to arrest Ortiz and Archuleta proved unsuccessful, and these rebels have, without doubt, escaped in the direction of Chihuahua."

Price, however, also noted that after "the flight of Ortiz and Archuleta, the rebellion appeared to be suppressed; but this appearance was deceptive." Indeed it was. In January 1847, what became known as the Taos Rebellion erupted when Governor Bent traveled to his home in Taos to be with his family. A few days later, a group of insurgents attacked Bent. He was killed and scalped, and his body was dragged through the streets. A mob gathered, and five others were killed as some of the survivors fled to Santa Fe.

In response, Colonel Price headed north with 353 soldiers and volunteers to quash the uprising. En route, the troops encountered a force of fifteen hundred insurgents at Santa Cruz de la Cañada, just south of Los Luceros. Price was outnumbered, but he had four twelve-pounder mountain howitzers. In the battle that followed, Price's command lost only two men, while killing thirty-six rebels and forcing the insurgents to retreat.

Price followed their tracks up the Río Grande. When they reached Los Luceros on January 27, they pitched tents in the dormant fields and waited for reinforcements before pressing on to the north. Price's men conducted a perfunctory search for Diego Archuleta, knowing the odds of his being there were slim to none.

The next day, the additional troops arrived, more dragoons as well as Company A, Second Regiment, Missouri Mounted Volunteers, under the command of Lieutenant Nathan Boone, the youngest son of legendary frontiersman Daniel Boone.

On January 29, Price's force, now comprising 479 rank-and-file soldiers, departed their staging ground at Los Luceros. Before leaving, Price, in an act of pure vengeance, ordered Archuleta's residence torched and burned to ashes, destroying what was said to be the finest library in New Mexico.

"On the 29th I marched to La Joya [present-day Velarde], where I learned that a party of sixty or eighty of the enemy had posted themselves on the steep slopes

Horse wagon at Los Luceros. Gilbert Vigil collection, courtesy of Marie Markesteyn.

of the mountains which rise on each side of the cañon, or gorge, which leads to Embudo," Price later wrote.

The rocky walls and icy slopes of the constricted gorge made the Battle of Embudo Pass especially challenging. When the smoke cleared, Price's infantry and dragoons had prevailed, with only one soldier killed and one badly wounded. The insurgents' losses came to twenty killed and sixty wounded. To this day, hikers taking the old trail from Velarde to Dixon traverse the battle site. On the large rocks in the pass, many crosses have been chipped over the years to mark spots where the defenders died.

After the fight at Embudo, the rebels retreated to Taos, and the American force tramped through deep snow in pursuit. Once they reached Taos, deadly cannon fire at point-blank range brought the three-week revolt to an end.

Later that year, a grand jury indicted twenty-nine instigators of the revolt for treason. Twenty-five of those indictments were dismissed for lack of evidence. One of the four not dismissed was Antonio María Trujillo, a resident of the Los Luceros settlement and father-in-law of Diego Archuleta. The seizure and imprisonment of the old man, held in high esteem by all who knew him, stunned the families of Los Luceros. When he was tried, convicted, and sentenced to death, his family and supporters sent a petition for pardon to Washington, DC. Ultimately, it was decided that Trujillo and all the others could not be prosecuted for treason because they were not yet citizens of the United States. All of them were granted pardons.

Archuleta returned to New Mexico, moved into a new home at Los Luceros, and took an oath of allegiance to the American government. He became involved in territorial politics and was elected to the New Mexico Territorial Legislative Assembly, where he served for many years. President Abraham Lincoln appointed Archuleta as an Indian agent in New Mexico, and in 1862, during the Civil War, he became the first Hispanic promoted to the rank of brigadier general.

Much like the old warrior Diego Archuleta, the citizens of the Río Arriba gradually adjusted to the acquisition of New Mexico by the United States. Under the rule of the new American territorial government, Los Luceros functioned as the seat of government of the newly formed Río Arriba County, one of the seven original counties of New Mexico. There was no official courthouse or jail. Rooms were rented in private residences for legal hearings and trials. According to early county records, between 1848 and 1851, District Court proceedings were held at Los Luceros in "the house of Don Julián Lucero." Records indicate that in later years, court at Plaza de Los Luceros also was held at the homes of brothers Diego and Pantaleón Archuleta.

In 1848, one of the more colorful characters to take part in a trial at Lucero's home was the notorious María Gertrudis Barceló, New Mexico's celebrated gambler and courtesan. Often called Doña Tules, or simply La Tules, this bold and independent spirit brought suit against George W. Coulter, proprietor of the United States Hotel, also known as the Fonda and later the Exchange Hotel on the Santa Fe Plaza. The lawsuit alleged that Coulter failed to repay a $500 loan he had received from La Tules to cover a gambling debt. After an all-Anglo jury in Santa Fe was unable to reach a verdict, La Tules's attorneys won a change of venue. In April 1850, the trial was moved to Río Arriba County and convened at Los Luceros. A new jury of local residents quickly found in favor of La Tules. Four years later, she died, bequeathing a substantial fortune to the church and several charities.

On April 26, 1850, the other big news at Los Luceros was the marriage of Julián Lucero's daughter María Marta Lucero to Elias Zachary Clark, an Irish-born trader and merchant from Missouri. The bride was thirty years old and her groom was thirty-five, advanced ages at that time for newlyweds. That November,

Maria Marta. Courtesy of Marie Markesteyn.

Julián Lucero, a recently widowed, eighty-year-old, major property owner, deeded his main house in the "town of Los Luceros" to the couple: "in consideration of the love and affection he bears to his daughter." The gift included all the furnishings in the house, the orchard just to the south, and a tract of land on the west side of the Río Grande. Lucero asked his daughter and son-in-law to give up all rights to his other houses and agree to take care of him in his final years. In 1853, just before he died, he deeded the Clarks more apple, peach, and apricot orchards in return for paying his funeral expenses, which they did.

Much as Julián Lucero had done for many years, Clark bought as much property as he could in and near the community of Los Luceros. Soon his holdings by purchase and inheritance included a gristmill that had belonged to his father-in-law and many more houses and orchards. For the next decade, the Clarks continued to enlarge their land holdings. Clark ranched and farmed and, with help from his brother, Louis Clark, operated a general merchandise store in the nearby village of Alcalde.

The apples, pears, and peaches of the lower Chama and La Joya long ago gave Río Arriba a place among the horticulture districts of the Southwest. The first irrigation ditches on American soil were constructed hereabouts and at Los Luceros and Plaza Alcalde; and the first apples and pears produced in the Rocky Mountain region were grown here; indeed, at Los Luceros is a notable pear tree that has yielded fruit for more than two hundred years, and is undoubtedly the first tree of this variety of fruit planted in the United States.

—NEW MEXICO GOVERNOR MIGUEL OTERO, 1901

Clark also became involved in politics and government. He served as probate clerk for Río Arriba County, and in 1851, he was named clerk of the US District Court for the Second Judicial District of the Territory of New Mexico. Two years later, the council of the legislative assembly in Santa Fe selected Clark to be their clerk, a post he held through the 1853–1856 terms. In 1857, the governor commissioned Clark territorial treasurer.

During this period, Los Luceros earned its reputation for graciousness and hospitality. In 1855, W. W. H. Davis, US Attorney for the Territory of New Mexico, who later became acting governor, wrote in glowing terms of his visit to Los Luceros:

We continued up the valley until nearly dark, when we arrived at the hospitable ranch of Mr. Clark, at Los Luceros, where we stopped for the night. He welcomed us with genuine hospitality. We were ushered into the sala, where we found a cheerful fire blazing upon the hearth, which put new life into our benumbed bodies. For me the ride was unusually fatiguing, and when I dismounted it was with difficulty that I could walk into the house. For the first time I had backed a Mexican saddle, which, though pleasant to ride upon when you have become accustomed to them, generally punish the uninitiated for a few days. I thought to myself that, if thus crippled in the first day's ride, there would be nothing of me left long before the circuit should be completed. In a little while supper was announced, when we were seated at a well-filled board, presided over by Mrs. Clark in person, contrary to the general custom of Mexican ladies, who do not eat with their guests. Soon after, the colchones [mattresses] were spread upon the floor, when we retired, and slept soundly until morning.

In the morning, the Davis party pressed on to Taos. In only a few busy days, Davis not only fulfilled his legal duties but also attended a lively baile, or ball, and made the acquaintance of Kit Carson, whom he found "quiet and unassuming."

After the docket was cleared and court adjourned, Davis headed south for another stay at Los Luceros. "We rode leisurely down the valley," Davis wrote, "and just before dark arrived at the rancho of Mr. Clark, where we were again welcomed with his accustomed hospitality. I remained at Los Luceros until the following Monday morning, and passed a quiet and not unpleasant Sabbath under the hospitable roof of Mr. Clark."

Davis's assessment of Los Luceros and the generosity of the Clarks was similar to that of most guests who stayed there. In 1859, one of Abraham Lincoln's close friends, Judge John S. Watts, a lawyer and former judge of the territorial courts, paused at Los Luceros with his son, John Watts. "This morning we rose quite early and rode along the Rio Grande ten miles for breakfast at a friend's of my father— Mr. Clark—he has quite a pretty place on the Rio Grande—the place he lives in is called Los Luceros," the younger Watts wrote in his journal for September 29.

In 1860, Elias Clark, the gracious *patrón* of Los Luceros, died, probably of tuberculosis, at the age of forty-five. His brother, Louis, took over the dry goods store at Alcalde and lent support to his widowed sister-in-law. In 1876, a disgruntled customer shot and killed Louis Clark when he was denied credit at the store. By then, the Los Luceros property had passed to Eliza Clark, born in 1848, the only living child of Elias and María Marta Clark. A son, Luis Clark, had died at birth in 1851.

Only nine years old at the time of her father's death, Eliza married a young farmer named Luis M. Ortiz in 1866 when she was barely thirteen. Like his young wife, eighteen-year-old Ortiz came from a distinguished family that had arrived in New Mexico as colonists with Diego de Vargas at the time of the Reconquest in 1693. He was descended from the Martín Serrano family through both of his parents, Don Gaspar Ortiz, an officer in the Mexican army during the war with the United States, and María Magdalena Lucero, who was related through blood to the illustrious Sebastián Martín.

Gaspar Ortiz and his wife lived at Los Luceros for a few years after their marriage and the birth of their oldest son, Luis, in 1848. Gaspar Ortiz owned and operated a store, and the family home was near the residences of Diego Archuleta and Julián Lucero. Later, Gaspar Ortiz settled in Santa Fe, where he became a prosperous freighter, operated a mercantile store, and twice served as Santa Fe County probate judge.

Young Luis Ortiz remained at Los Luceros and farmed the land, seemingly with great success. By 1870, county records indicate that he was one of the wealthiest residents of the precinct of Los Luceros. According to the 1870 federal census, Luis

Luis and Eliza Ortiz. Courtesy of Marie Markesteyn.

Ortiz was twenty-two, and Eliza was sixteen. They had a three-year-old daughter, Teresa, and employed a Navajo cook, Guadalupe, who lived in the household
with her four small children. The value of their estate was impressive for the
time, as was the family's livestock, which included horses, mules, oxen, cattle,
and hogs. The Ortiz orchards were productive, the vineyards yielded hundreds of
gallons of wine, and the fields produced bumper crops of spring wheat, Indian
corn, and beans.

During the many years the Ortiz family lived at Los Luceros, they not only
maintained the hacienda but also made improvements, just as Eliza's father, Elias
Clark, had done when he managed the property. It is sometimes difficult to dis-
tinguish exactly who is responsible for some of the architectural changes. Even
in death, Clark remains at the center of at least two of the many continuing Los
Luceros debates. On one side are those who insist that not one scintilla of proof
exists that Clark served as a district court judge. Others hold not only that Clark was
a judge for a brief period but also that he held court in the second-floor sala, or par-
lor, of the Casa Grande and supposedly converted a nearby building into a jailhouse.

The claim that Clark used the upper-story sala for a courtroom is the subject of the other ongoing debate. Those who question the validity of Clark's judge-ship also doubt that the second story of the Casa Grande was added while Clark was alive. In part, they credit the expansion to the Ortiz family that followed the Clarks as owners, based on the writings of US Attorney Davis. Although he had been the guest of the Clarks for several days, Davis did not mention a second floor when he described the comforts of the sala.

Taken out of context, it has been natural to identify the large, second-floor room at the front of the present main house at Los Luceros as the sala into which Davis and party were ushered by the Clarks. It is unlikely, however, that the novelty of a two-story home with a center-hall plan would have escaped Davis's notice, or that he would not have painfully acknowledged a necessity to climb stairs in his Mexican-saddle-induced "crippled" condi-tion. Clark may have remodeled one of the buildings in Los Luceros into a center-hall plan and built upwards after 1853, but this is unlikely in the early Territorial period when milled lumber was a scarce, expensive commodity only recently available at all, and second stories remained rare even in Santa Fe. His death in 1860 precluded further possibilities.

—DR. CORRINE P. SZE, *HISTORY OF THE LOS LUCEROS RANCH*

Other sources offer no definitive information about credit for the improvements and structural changes made at Casa Grande. "It is also possible that Eliza and Luis Ortiz were responsible for some of the Territorial Style remodeling to the ranch house, in the late 1860s or the 1870s," wrote Betsy Swanson in the nomination of Los Luceros to National Register of Historic Places. "Structural evidence indicates a series of renovations in the Greek Revival Style and local tradition attributes remodelings to both Elias Clark and Luis Ortiz."

Besides supervising improvements to the family home and running a farm and ranch, Ortiz tended to his civic obligations and entered politics. In 1882, he was a member of three committees while serving as one of two elected represen-tatives of Río Arriba County in the Territorial Legislature. Later, he held other positions in Río Arriba County, including county clerk, county assessor, court recorder, and both clerk and recorder of the probate court. In 1887, Ortiz became the sheriff of Río Arriba County, serving a single two-year term before returning to Los Luceros to devote his time exclusively to his agricultural business.

By the mid-1890s, the Ortiz family included four more children—Gaspar, Cleotilde, Marie Beatrice, and Louisa—and six persons listed on the census only as "Indians." With assistance from these Navajo "family members," Eliza tended to visitors and the needs of her children. The couple also continued to update the property, such as adding a Territorial Style gallery encircling the second story of the main house.

The Ortiz family built a private chapel—originally named the Chapel of the Holy Family and now called Capilla de Nuestra Señora de Guadalupe (Chapel of Our Lady of Guadalupe)—on the grounds near their home to show gratitude after the house survived a flood in 1886. Many locals believed it was erected near the site of the original eighteenth-century chapel. Eliza and Luis Ortiz donated the *capilla* (chapel) and some of the land surrounding it to the Archdiocese of Santa Fe in 1891, under the express condition that it be used for religious purposes only. The couple lies buried beneath the floor of the altar.

Soon after the turn of the twentieth century, Abel Lucero built a late-Victorian–style cottage on two tracts his father deeded to him just east of the impressive manse of his first cousin, Luis Ortiz. It was adobe with a pitched roof, front and side porches, and a good well just outside the kitchen door. A mulberry tree that produced white berries grew in the front yard, and another mulberry tree east of the porch bore dark blue berries. Both shade trees still stand, with massive trunks scarred by ice and time, supplying berries for pies, jelly, and generation after generation of hungry birds.

After a two-year term as territorial auditor ended in 1901, Ortiz left public service and spent his time with family and friends at Los Luceros. After the death of his wife, Eliza, in 1909, he remained in the Casa Grande with two of his daughters and three servants. When New Mexico achieved statehood in 1912, Ortiz was actively trying to sell all his Los Luceros property. He soon found interested parties. Clara D. True, Mary T. Bryan, and Felix Martínez purchased the property in 1912 with a mortgage payable in three years for the purchase price of $10,000 at 8 percent interest.

True, who devoted fifty years of her life working as a reformer on behalf of Indian tribes, had taught school at Santa Clara Pueblo before moving away for two years to aid California tribes. In spite of her good works, True was contemptuous of Indian people and believed all of them to be childlike and incompetent. She was quoted by Margaret D. Jacobs as saying, "Few of the [Indian] people I am to spend time with seem more interesting or spiritual than a brickbat, yet they are said to have souls. . . . I'll see if I can get enough of them sober at once to experiment with."

True moved back to New Mexico in 1910 and settled in the Española Valley, where she owned and operated several ranches. Mary Bryan, who some people erroneously believed was True's sister, became her partner. Bryan, as True put it, was a "woman of wealth and position." But neither the materialistic True, who earned the moniker The Devil of the Río Grande, nor the supposedly wealthy Bryan could keep up the mortgage payments for Los Luceros. After four years of litigation in Río Arriba County District Court, the mortgage was foreclosed. Ortiz, who was then living with a daughter and her family, repossessed Los Luceros, but no one was taking care of the property. Left unattended, the big house slowly deteriorated as rains seeped through the roof and soaked the adobe walls. Flooding from the acequia did more damage, and vandals broke windows and stripped away some of the woodwork. It appeared that the end was at hand for Los Luceros.

Then, in the early 1920s, a ray of hope appeared. A woman from an aristocratic Boston family came to the rescue of the sagging property on the Río Grande. Mary Cabot Wheelwright, a patron of the arts looking for a bit of adventure, purchased Los Luceros.

Following spread: "Jail"/old garage

Above: Capilla de Nuestra Señora de Guadalupe
Opposite: Casa Grande

Grand Sala fireplace featuring Olive Rush
frescoes, Casa Grande

67

Top: Grand Sala in Casa Grande
Bottom: Casa Grande dining room

Top: Casa Grande kitchen
Bottom: Casa Grande dining room

Left: Olive Rush frescoes on kiva fireplace in Casa Grande bedroom

Right: Haunted stairway in Casa Grande

Opposite: Capilla de Nuestra Señora de Guadalupe featuring altar and art by Clare Villa

Mary Cabot Wheelwright and Amigo at Los Luceros, autumn 1924. Mary Cabot
Wheelwright Collection, Album XIV, Wheelwright Museum of the American Indian, Santa Fe.

6   The Wheelwright Era

It seems improbable that a middle-aged blueblood spinster from New England became the savior of Los Luceros, but that is precisely what happened. Mary Cabot Wheelwright's timing was perfect and entirely serendipitous.

Born in 1878, Mary Wheelwright was the only child of a family from the highest echelon of upper-class Boston. Her father, Andrew Cunningham Wheelwright, was a prosperous Harvard-educated merchant descended from early Massachusetts settlers, and her mother, Sarah Perkins Cabot, known as Sadie, was a fifth-generation member of one of the first families of Boston. The Cabots were successful eighteenth-century merchants whose ships carried profitable cargoes of rum, opium, and slaves. Over time, the family elevated its social status by marrying into other wealthy families and accumulating immense fortunes in the more conventional shipping business.

As the only child of protective parents, Wheelwright had few playmates. The loneliness of her secluded childhood is evident in a portrait of her painted when she was four years old by Frank Duveneck. It shows an expressionless little girl holding her small doll, with a discarded rose on the floor. The original oil portrait is in the Brooklyn Museum, but a handsomely framed copy hangs in the second-floor sala of the Casa Grande.

Like other young ladies of wealth at that time and place, Wheelwright received her formal education from tutors and governesses and at exclusive girls' schools in private homes. She studied art and classical music and excelled at voice and piano, but her passions were horseback riding and sailing, an activity that would have pleased her Cabot ancestors. She knew some of the area's leading citizens. Her mother regaled her with stories of social encounters with President Grover Cleveland, philosopher Bronson Alcott, the father of novelist Louisa May Alcott, and Senator Charles Sumner, a powerful orator and abolitionist.

In 1904, Sadie Wheelwright presented her daughter with a ninety-five-page typescript memoir entitled *Reminiscences*, describing her meetings with two of the giants of the Transcendentalist movement of the mid-nineteenth century—Henry David Thoreau, the author of *Walden*, and Ralph Waldo Emerson, a frequent guest in the Cabot home whose biographer was Sadie's older brother James Elliot Cabot.

Tall, thin, and somewhat awkward, Mary had few suitors and little chance of marriage. As was the custom for unwed daughters, she was obliged to care for her aging parents. Each summer, she accompanied them on sailing jaunts along the coasts of Maine and Nova Scotia, with occasional trips to California and France. After her father's death in 1908, Wheelwright and her mother visited Greece, Egypt, and other foreign lands.

In December 1917, her widowed mother passed away, and Wheelwright's parental obligation ended. Although she had been close to her mother and grieved her death, the dutiful Victorian daughter was now free to travel wherever she wanted to go. As the sole heir of a substantial fortune, she was guaranteed a significant income for the rest of her life, although her father, wary of fortune hunters, had ensured that his daughter had no direct access to her money but regularly received a generous stipend from the family trust. Even with this financial limitation, Wheelwright could then live life on her own terms. In some ways, she felt her life was just beginning, as she wrote later in her unpublished autobiography.

"I think one of the secrets of happiness is to do as the Indians do, live simply at the time, not worrying about the future, doing the best they know how at that moment," she later wrote. "At any rate, in middle life when my parents had died, I came West. Not merely to California which I had seen superficially, but to the Southwest where I seemed to get near to something I had always wanted, a more simple type of civilization, more adventuresome and more exciting than the safety of Boston."

Wheelwright, accompanied by her traveling companion, Katie Scott, was two months short of her fortieth birthday when she first visited New Mexico in the spring of 1918. After arriving at the small village of Lamy on a westbound Atchison, Topeka and Santa Fe train, the two women boarded another train that shuttled them eighteen miles north to Santa Fe on a spur line. They spent a night in what Wheelwright described only as a "very bad Santa Fe hotel."

The next morning, a handsome cowboy wearing tooled boots, a big Tom Mix–style hat, and a wide grin met them in the lobby. Once their trunks had been loaded into a touring car, they drove northeast out of Santa Fe. They motored thirty miles to the Pajarito Plateau, a sprawling formation of volcanic rock canyons and mesas on the east flank of the Jemez Mountains. Once they crossed the Río Grande on a rickety bridge, the big car climbed a steep mesa to their destination, the Rancho Ramón Vigil.

Richard and Carol Pfaffle, managers of the guest ranch, warmly welcomed Wheelwright and Scott and showed them to one of the cabins that would be their home for April and May of 1918, at a cost of twenty-one dollars a week, including meals. Wheelwright's choice of Rancho Ramón Vigil for lodging was not random. She was well acquainted with Carol Pfaffle.

Her name had been Caroline Bishop Stanley when she was born north of Boston in the resort town of Nahant in 1879, one year after Wheelwright's birth. Carol had had an older brother who died during childbirth, and her twin brother, Edward, lived only two months. Like Wheelwright, Carol was raised as an only child in an old and established Massachusetts family related to such well-known families as the Choates, Perkinses, and probably the Cabots. The Stanleys were comfortable, but not nearly as wealthy as the Boston Brahmins.

Also like Wheelwright, Carol was drawn to music at an early age. A few years after graduating from Boston's New England Conservatory of Music in 1905, she developed a friendship with Wheelwright while working as a volunteer at the South End Music Settlement School in Boston, founded in 1910 by Wheelwright as a cultural resource primarily for immigrant children.

Carol Stanley enjoyed teaching music and playing piano professionally for the pleasure of the well-heeled vacationers summering at Nahant, but she also dreamed of doing more than spending her life as an old maid in her family's home. When her wealthy grandmother, Almira Choate Johnson, died, she left Carol a large residence just across the street from the poet Henry Wadsworth Longfellow's summer home and a sizable monetary inheritance. With her sudden financial security and after an unhappy love affair, Carol left town. She briefly lived in Chicago, but when close friends told her about the natural beauty and enticing lifestyle of the Southwest, she packed a bag, bought a train ticket, and went to see the exotic land for herself.

Carol traveled around New Mexico, Arizona, and Utah. She stayed with friends and met archaeologists, writers, and her first genuine "cowboys and Indians." She learned to sit astride a horse in a western saddle and took part in camping expeditions and long rides across the high desert and throughout the canyon lands. She briefly returned to Chicago, but by 1916, she was back in New Mexico and settled in at the Hotel De Vargas in Santa Fe, and she never looked back.

That year, following a three-week-long guided trail ride from Santa Fe to Chaco Canyon and Canyon de Chelly, one of the cowboy guides caught Carol's eye. She married Richard Leroy Pfaffle on October 2 in Gallup, New Mexico. She was thirty-six, and Roy, as everyone called him, was three years younger. They returned to Santa Fe just long enough to pack their belongings and move to Española, a highway and railroad town south of Los Luceros in Río Arriba County.

In 1917, the Pfaffles launched a guided outfitting business at the Oñate Hotel in Española, catering to affluent Americans who canceled their trips abroad because of America's entry into World War I. It was a bit of a risk because through poor management of her family finances, Carol had lost much of the money she had inherited. However, the outfitting business was so good that the ambitious couple took on the management of the Pajarito Club, the name of a guest ranch soon to be changed to Rancho Ramón Vigil. Charles Lummis, a journalist and an activist for Indian rights and historic preservation, was a guest on two occasions in December 1917. During the winter and spring of 1918, as the war raged in Europe, the main lodge and cabins were constantly booked. Eldridge Adams, the Pfaffles' business adviser, checked in with an entourage that included members of both the Rothschild and Rockefeller families.

By the time Wheelwright and her companion found their way to the ranch, Carol and Roy Pfaffle were poised to take on the management of yet another ranch property. James Thorpe, a Denver mining mogul, purchased a sizable tract of land in the Sangre de Cristo foothills of Tesuque, north of Santa Fe. Named Bishop's Ranch, the property included the chapel and retreat once used by Archbishop Jean-Baptiste Lamy, the French Jesuit whose story had inspired Willa Cather's novel *Death Comes for the Archbishop*. Anxious to open his own guest ranch, Thorpe approached the Pfaffles and asked them to manage the property, which he renamed Bishop's Lodge. The Pfaffles accepted Thorpe's offer.

They were confident that they could oversee the Tesuque property and still maintain their outfitting business in Española and the guest ranch on the Pajarito Plateau. A major factor in their decision was the reality that because of an exceptionally dry winter, the water wells on the plateau were almost dry. During Wheelwright's stay at the ranch, water had to be hauled in. Oblivious to the situation, Wheelwright was fascinated by the landscape and the variety of people she encountered. She had a sense of freedom in this place where family and wealth seemed unimportant.

In late April, at about the halfway point of Wheelwright's stay at Rancho Ramón Vigil, the owner of the ranch managed to sell it to Frank Bond, a powerful sheep rancher and entrepreneur. The Pfaffles continued to work at the ranch for Bond for a few weeks, but by the end of May when Wheelwright returned to Boston, they had moved, along with most of the ranch hands and trail guides, to Bishop's Lodge. In Santa Fe, Pfaffle met a young cowboy named Everett Vey "Jack" Lambert. Born in Okarche, Oklahoma, the twenty-year-old had already worked as a cowhand, camp cook, and trail guide, including a stint at the legendary 101 Ranch in Oklahoma. He was driving a taxi in Santa Fe and jumped at the chance to return to ranch life and long trail rides when Pfaffle offered him a job at Bishop's Lodge.

At first, life in Tesuque was sweet for the Pfaffles. A steady stream of guests checked into the cabins. Some saddled up for horseback expeditions led by Pfaffle and Lambert; some opted for auto tours of scenic sites in the region. Carol Pfaffle oversaw the daily ranch operations, and when her husband surprised her with a grand piano for an anniversary gift, she entertained guests and offered piano lessons to friends and local children. Before long, however, Pfaffle's bad habits began to take a toll on his professional and personal relationships. If there was anything he enjoyed more than riding, it was high-stakes poker. When his gambling became a full-blown addiction, so did his habitual consumption of strong drink.

In late 1919, James Thorpe, owner of Bishop's Lodge, fired Pfaffle from his post as ranch manager. Thorpe accused him of mismanagement, even though the ranch was doing quite well and turning a hefty profit. Pfaffle's gambling and drinking might have played a part in his disgrace. In addition, it was rumored that Pfaffle and his pal Jack Lambert were quietly hunting for funds to buy a guest ranch of their own. The rumors proved true. With help from a lawyer, the Pfaffles and Lambert had found some land for sale that looked promising.

The thirty-four-thousand-acre tract was in the village of Alcalde, just a few miles north of Española. On the east side of the Río Grande, the land was bordered by San Juan Pueblo property to the south and the fields and orchards of Los Luceros to the east. The land was owned by the family of Elias Clark, who had been six years old in 1876 when his father, Louis Clark, was murdered in his mercantile store. Elias was the nephew and namesake of the Elias Clark who had been a previous owner of Los Luceros.

After procuring loans from family members and friends as well as a few private investors, the Pfaffles' purchase of the Alcalde land was completed in February 1920. They faced a lot of work. Some derelict adobe buildings on the property had to be refurbished, the old hacienda renovated, and corrals built. They named their new guest ranch San Gabriel in honor of the nearby first capital of New Mexico.

One of the first guests at San Gabriel was Mary Wheelwright, who returned to New Mexico in 1920 for an extended stay. San Gabriel offered a convenient base for her explorations of the greater Southwest. From San Gabriel, Wheelwright traveled the Río Arriba region and far beyond on horseback, usually accompanied by Jack Lambert, who later recalled that there was "no pavement, and not one fence between [San Gabriel] and Gallup or the Grand Canyon."

"My particular release and joy in the East was sailing and cruising on the sea in summer, and when I came to the desert I found it gave me a similar feeling of vastness and escape, and I came to love that, too," Wheelwright wrote in her auto-

San Gabriel Dude Ranch, 1920s. Courtesy of Marie Markesteyn.

biography of her travels in New Mexico. "I rode a great deal and that was how I came to know the Navaho and their reservation."

On a visit to the Navajo reservation during her 1921 stay at San Gabriel, Wheelwright—along with her friend Evelyn Sears, Carol Pfaffle, and their driver, Orville Cox—attended the first Gallup Inter Tribal Indian Ceremonial. Among the many displays of pottery, jewelry, rugs, and carvings, she came upon a striking ceremonial sand-painting tapestry titled *Hail Chant*. It had been woven by Hosteen Klah, a respected Navajo singer, or medicine man, as well as an accomplished weaver. Wheelwright purchased the weaving and tucked it away in her luggage.

A few days later, the party stopped south of Shiprock, New Mexico, at a remote trading post operated by Arthur and Frances ("Franc") Newcomb, who told them that their friend Klah was leading a Yeibichai, or Night Chant ceremony, that evening. Wheelwright was anxious to attend in spite of the stormy weather. She hoped to meet the creator of her new weaving.

The chemistry was instant between Klah and Mary Wheelwright. As author Lesley Poling-Kempes would later write, "their friendship seemed preordained in both their lives." Wheelwright was impressed with Klah and fully supportive of his mission to protect his Native religion and culture by weaving depictions of ceremonial sand-painting figures. He would become her teacher, and she would devote herself to preserving Navajo rituals. Wheelwright and Klah remained fast friends and collaborators for many years to come.

In the autumn of 1923, two years after her first meeting with Hosteen Klah, Wheelwright made another life-changing discovery. She found Los Luceros. Wheelwright and Carol Pfaffle were riding through the bosque beneath the big cottonwoods with shimmering golden leaves when off to the east, they saw a cluster of adobe buildings. The women turned their horses and slowed them to a trot. As they drew near, it was evident that the place had been abandoned. The buildings had been vacant for years. Stands of weeds covered what had once been flower beds and a vegetable garden. The orchards were overgrown, and the trees lining the dirt road bristled with dead limbs.

Carol explained that this was the Los Luceros Ranch and that she and her husband were the owners. In January, they had purchased 138 acres of fields and orchards, the Casa Grande, and all the other buildings from Louis Ortiz and his family. The deed was in the safe at San Gabriel. The Pfaffles had bought the ranch to grow alfalfa and to pasture the growing remuda of San Gabriel horses. They had no intention of restoring the hacienda or any of the outbuildings.

Top: Chapel at Los Luceros. Mary Cabot Wheelwright Collection, Album XIV, Wheelwright Museum of the American Indian, Santa Fe.

Bottom: Horses at Casa Grande and Mary Cabot Wheelwright on balcony, Los Luceros, 1923. Mary Cabot Wheelwright Collection, Album XIV, Wheelwright Museum of the American Indian, Santa Fe.

Wheelwright asked to see inside the main house. They tethered their horses to a picket fence and pushed open a side door. When their eyes adjusted to the dim light, they could see the piles of manure left by livestock that had entered the house. The forty-two-inch-thick adobe walls of the first floor were in poor condition because of flooding from the Río Grande. It was not safe to step onto the rotting porches wrapped around the second floor.

Despite its shabby appearance, Mary Wheelwright fell in love with the place. By the time she and Carol Pfaffle rode back to the corrals at San Gabriel, she had convinced herself that Los Luceros must be hers. In a matter of days, she made a deal with the Pfaffles. Purportedly for $2,300, Wheelwright purchased six acres of land on the Río Grande that included the Casa Grande, a small building to the northwest, and an orchard.

Before departing from San Gabriel that autumn, Wheelwright arranged for Carol Pfaffle to supervise a complete renovation of the main house and the conversion of the smaller building into a garage. Carol agreed and made Ted Peabody, a skilled builder from Española who had helped to renovate San Gabriel Ranch, her construction foreman. During the renovation process, Carol moved into the guesthouse, an L-shaped adobe built in about 1900.

Peabody and his crew started with the Casa Grande. They repaired the leaky roof, replaced broken windows, and rebuilt the damaged walls. Following Wheelwright's instructions, Carol directed Peabody to add bay windows to the first-floor walls to provide more sunlight. Closets, rarely found in older adobe homes, were carved out of the interior walls in the bedrooms. The workers also built in bookshelves and cabinets and put corner fireplaces in most of the rooms on both floors. The corner fireplace in the southwest corner bedroom and the large fireplace on the west wall in the sala were adorned with decorative frescoes painted by noted Santa Fe artist Olive Rush, one of Wheelwright's close friends and a frequent visitor to Los Luceros. The Territorial wooden porches with French doors were repaired, and heavy plank doors with wrought-iron hardware were installed on the bedroom entries. A bathroom and a small but cozy library were created out of a large existing room on the second floor.

The flagstone walkways and small duck pond that Wheelwright requested were added, and an exterior staircase on the south side of the house was replaced by a sturdy interior staircase on the west wall of the entry hall. A mirador, or lookout, constructed on the roof turned out to be so heavy that the second-story ceilings began to sag. It was removed, and only the handsome wooden staircase to

After Mary Cabot Wheelwright's remodel of Casa Grande.
Courtesy of Marie Markesteyn.

the roof was left. All the doors and window trim were painted dark green, and the outside walls of the hacienda were whitewashed instead of being swathed in stucco.

The picket fence across the front yard was replaced by a low adobe wall, and the building just northwest of the Casa Grande, which many people still refer to as the "jail," was converted into a combination garage, coal bin, and workshop.

After more than a year of intensive labor, Carol Pfaffle and her foreman declared the job complete. Wheelwright was delighted with the makeover when she returned to make a final inspection. She approved of the Spanish Colonial and Pueblo Revival–style influences that were coming into vogue at the time. She also was pleased that much of the ranch house, including the two-level gallery and interior woodwork, retained the architectural integrity from the Territorial Period of the late nineteenth century, according to Betsy Swanson's National Register of Historic Places nomination form.

Wheelwright was never happier than when she was at Los Luceros. Over a span of thirty-five years, from 1923 until her death in 1958, Wheelwright visited Los Luceros once or twice a year, staying for a month or two and occasionally three. In 1943, she resided at Los Luceros from January until mid-October.

She preferred to visit in the fall or spring. A few times, she came out during the Christmas holidays and daily went to nearby San Gabriel to have dinner, play cards, or go for a long ride through the fields with some of the Pfaffles' guests.

Besides caring for the neglected buildings, Wheelwright tended to the fields, orchards, and gardens. In the yard surrounding the main house, she planted lilacs, a New Mexico favorite ever since the blooming shrubs had arrived with merchants journeying down the Santa Fe Trail. Wheelwright also acquired samplings of historic plants, including English roses and hollyhocks from the decorative garden laid out in the 1800s at the famed El Zaguán, an architectural treasure on Canyon Road in Santa Fe. Incarnations of the past survive. Peony bushes imported from China in the nineteenth century flourished for at least a few years of the twenty-first century at Los Luceros.

When in residence at Los Luceros, Wheelwright spent most mornings in her second-floor bedroom in the southeast corner, where her breakfast was brought to her every morning. Later, she took care of correspondence and read in the library on the west side or the sala that stretched across the front of the house. The views were good in all directions. Outside her south-facing bedroom windows were two enormous willows planted in the nineteenth century. Beyond the fence stretched the pastures, crop fields, and orchards.

Landscape at Los Luceros. Photograph by Cady Wells, June 1941. Mary Cabot Wheelwright Collection, Album XIV, Wheelwright Museum of the American Indian, Santa Fe.

Downstairs, the servants stayed in the rooms on the east side of the hallway across from the dining room, kitchen, and commissary, or pantry. Wheelwright presided at many luncheons and dinners in the dining room, but it was said that in all the time she lived at Los Luceros, she never once entered the kitchen. Along the wall between the pantry and a side door to the outside was a series of dog beds where Wheelwright's beloved Lhasa Apso terriers were tucked in each evening. The Lhasas could be moody and mischievous but were Wheelwright's favorite companions. She was particularly fond of Tai-Tai, a dog she acquired in China and brought to Los Luceros for breeding. Several of her Lhasas brought home show ribbons, and some pups were given as gifts to special friends.

In an interview with the author, "My brother Max and I worked at Los Luceros when we were just kids," recalled Gilbert Vigil, whose father, Max Vigil, was one of Wheelwright's top hands and trail guides. "Our job was to take care of those dogs. They were little, but they stood their ground. We loved them. Each dog had its own basket to sleep in and its own bowls. Every day, we'd feed and water them, and then we would all play on the lawn. They really needed to get exercise, so we'd walk them for a while. Miss Wheelwright would be upstairs and hear us coming back, and she'd go out and wave at us. She would call to the dogs and they'd yap at her, and she would laugh and laugh."

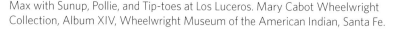

Max with Sunup, Pollie, and Tip-toes at Los Luceros. Mary Cabot Wheelwright Collection, Album XIV, Wheelwright Museum of the American Indian, Santa Fe.

Ranch hand on horse at Los Luceros, 1923. Mary Cabot Wheelwright Collection, Album XIV, Wheelwright Museum of the American Indian, Santa Fe.

Wheelwright was rarely alone during her stays at Los Luceros. Besides a cook and housekeeper, various ranch mangers and hired hands were in her employ. She was a superb horsewoman, but she never learned to drive an automobile and had no need to learn. For the first twenty years of her life at Los Luceros, her chauffeur from back east, Albert Staples, and his wife, Tina, drove out to New Mexico well ahead of Wheelwright. They made sure everything was in order, and when Wheelwright stepped off the train at Lamy after the long trip from Boston, Staples was there to greet her. Staples always had the car gassed and ready to go at a moment's notice. He drove her to social functions, cultural events, and dinner parties in Taos and Santa Fe. On the Santa Fe trips, Wheelwright usually managed to work in a stop for some gourmet goodies, English marmalade, and pastries at Kaune's Market, a specialty grocer established in 1896 that offered everything from "dried beans to caviar." Staples also drove Wheelwright and her guests to Native dances and festivities in the area and as far away as Navajo country.

There was plenty of room in the Casa Grande to accommodate out-of-towners. To provide a degree of privacy, Wheelwright converted the adobe casita built as a foreman's residence into a comfortable guesthouse. As soon as the renovation work was completed and Wheelwright began her part-time residency in northern New Mexico, a variety of visitors regularly came to her ranch retreat. Many of them were guests and working cowboys she knew from the nearby San Gabriel Ranch. They often showed up for a cup of tea—a daily ritual—or a horseback ride with their hostess, who wore a woolen riding coat and trousers and a proper riding hat whenever she rode at the ranch. Her friends and family from back East were frequent guests, along with a steady flow of distinguished artists, writers, musicians, public figures, expatriates, and avant-garde intellectuals.

Among the guests at Los Luceros were Georgia O'Keeffe, Aldous Huxley, Thornton Wilder, William Penhallow Henderson and Alice Corbin Henderson, Carl Jung, Ansel Adams, Mary Austin, Leopold Stokowski, Elsie Clews Parsons, Willa Cather, Dorothy Brett, Andrew Dasburg, Oliver La Farge, and many others who greatly influenced today's perceptions of northern New Mexico. Some of them, such as O'Keeffe, the Hendersons, and Parsons, were frequent visitors. Most were part of the growing art colony in Santa Fe or the inner circle of art patron Mabel Dodge Luhan in Taos.

Prior to settling in Taos in 1917, Mabel Dodge, a wealthy heiress from Buffalo, presided over famous salons in Florence and Manhattan, discussing and debating the arts, politics, and topics of the time such as the ideas of Sigmund Freud, the struggle of the working classes, and the virtues of free love. In 1923, the year Wheelwright took control of Los Luceros, Mabel—already thrice married and with an impressive string of former lovers—wed Tony Lujan, a Taos Indian and her final husband. At about that time, Wheelwright and the Lujans met at a San Gabriel party hosted by their mutual friends the Pfaffles.

From the 1920s well into the 1950s, many of the celebrated artists and writers staying with the Lujans in Taos found their way to Los Luceros for afternoon tea, dinner, or a picnic in the bosque. The old rancho on the Río Grande became a restful getaway from the spectacles that often resulted during high-octane gatherings tinged with drama at Los Gallos, Mabel's home in Taos.

One of Mabel's visitors was English poet and novelist D. H. Lawrence, who stayed in Taos three times between 1922 and 1925. Sometime before departing New Mexico for the last time, Lawrence came to Los Luceros, no doubt accompanied by the trio of women who constantly vied for his attention—his wife, Frieda, Mabel Dodge Luhan, and English painter Dorothy Brett. Wheelwright was thrilled to host her favorite author. Later, she became particularly fond of *Mornings in Mexico*, a collection of eight travel essays by Lawrence that were not published until after he had left New Mexico.

Picnic with friends at Los Luceros, October 1923. Handwriting on album page next to photograph: "Jack, Everett, Lois, R.L.P.[?], Carol, Mrs. P., H.S.[?], Peggie, L La B.[?]." Mary Cabot Wheelwright Collection, Album XIV, Wheelwright Museum of the American Indian, Santa Fe.

Besides *Mornings in Mexico*, several of Lawrence's other works, including an inscribed first edition of *The Plumed Serpent*, graced the bookcases in the Los Luceros guesthouse. More books lined the shelves in the snug library on the second floor of Casa Grande, including a prominent display of the *Complete Works of Theodore Roosevelt*. A friend and political confidante of various members of Wheelwright's family, Roosevelt had spent time in New Mexico as early as 1898 while recruiting cowboys for his Rough Rider regiment. He returned on several occasions for Rough Rider reunions, political missions, and tours of historical sites and natural landmarks in New Mexico and other locales in the Southwest. Just as D. H. Lawrence would later do, Roosevelt wrote about his experiences attending the Hopi snake and antelope dances.

"Several times we walked up the precipitous cliff trails to the mesa top, and visited three villages thereon," Roosevelt wrote in *A Book-Lover's Holidays in the Open* after his visit to Hopi in 1913. "We were received with friendly courtesy—perhaps partly because we endeavored to show good manners ourselves, which, I am sorry to say, is not invariably the case with tourists."

Wheelwright must have been pleased that two of the men she most admired, who seemingly had nothing in common, shared her interest in Indian culture.

Wheelwright's interest in tribal art, religion, and history had become an intense passion since her first encounter with Hosteen Klah in 1921. She admired Lawrence and Roosevelt, but Klah fascinated her. In just a few years, they not only established a close friendship but also became important forces in each other's lives.

When Klah was a boy, the Navajo elders recognized him as a male with feminine characteristics, making him a *nádleeh*—"one who changes" or "one who is transformed." According to tribal beliefs, such persons were special and held in high esteem. Klah, trained in the traditional female craft of weaving, became a master weaver and a revered medicine man. He was taught the healing power of herbs, learned chanting and sand painting, and studied the Navajo tribal ceremonies. By using his talents as a singer and weaver, Klah hoped to protect and save his people's sacred religious customs.

Wheelwright wanted to help her friend and had the means to do so. The preservation of the Navajo rituals and stories became her obsession. Eventually, Wheelwright devised a plan for preserving the traditional Navajo ceremonial ways so that they would not be lost forever. In the winter of 1927, a select group of people was summoned to Los Luceros. The visitors included Hosteen Klah and his nephew Clyde Beyal, the brother of Beaal Begay, Klah's young student. Art and Franc Newcomb, owners of the trading post where Wheelwright had begun her long Navajo journey, also came with their four-year-old daughter. A bulky recording machine was shipped to the ranch and a typist hired to write up Franc Newcomb's descriptions of the scores of sand paintings that accompanied Klah's chants.

For more than two months, the recording sessions continued, mostly in the sala of Casa Grande. Klah chanted into the recorder until he became so hoarse, he had to stop to rest. Wheelwright's chauffeur, Albert Staples, and his wife, Tina, looked after the guests and often drove Klah and the others to various pueblos to watch dances and meet the tribal governor and medicine men.

The Wheelwright-Klah collaboration continued for ten years. Klah wove massive tapestries of sand paintings, and Franc Newcomb painted her own watercolor versions of the sand paintings for posterity. Wheelwright faithfully recorded every word as Klah gave her the myths and many of the other important stories that are the foundation of the Navajo religion.

"I was anxious to record Klah's Creation Myth, feeling that I would have a basic understanding of his belief," Wheelwright wrote in her autobiography. "In 1930, in the spring I went to Santa Barbara, California, staying at San Ysidro Ranch and there in about ten days Klah told me the Creation Myth. He came

Hastiin Klah and Frances Newcomb, ca. 1935. (Possibly taken at Los Luceros.) Wheelwright Museum of the American Indian, Santa Fe.

with Arthur Newcomb and his nephew, Clyde Beyal, who was the interpreter. After that I tried to use him with Klah because it was the natural thing for a nephew to help his uncle ceremonially, and Clyde was an intelligent interpreter."

It was peaceful at San Ysidro, a luxury ranch resort nestled in the Montecito hills at the foot of the Santa Ynez Mountains. Like Los Luceros, it was originally part of a Spanish land grant. Over time, it became a sanctuary for Franciscan monks, a cattle ranch, a citrus farm, and finally, a resort for the rich and famous. The guest book bore the signatures of Winston Churchill, Somerset Maugham, John Galsworthy, Groucho Marx, Sinclair Lewis, and Bing Crosby.

The visit to California pleased Klah. He had longed to see the Pacific Ocean because in an episode in the Navajo Creation Myth, the revered deity Changing Woman had traveled far from Navajo country to live on an island off the California coast. Wheelwright took Klah to a local museum to view the various artifacts that had been excavated on the islands.

Carl Jung, the eminent psychiatrist, who visited New Mexico in 1924–1925, was supportive of the ongoing work of Wheelwright and Klah. After reading the first volume of the Navajo Creation Story, Jung offered his encouragement and praise. "He sent me a message that I had done a most valuable thing in collecting the source material," Wheelwright noted in her memoir.

Wheelwright's commitment to her work steadily increased. Besides meeting other tribal singers at ceremonials, Wheelwright sought counsel from Harold Bauer, the brilliant pianist who introduced the works of Maurice Ravel and Claude Debussy to American audiences, and the great conductor Leopold Stokowski. "I asked them if something should not be done to record the chants of the Navaho, which accompanied all their rituals, and they both urged that records be made if possible," Wheelwright wrote. "I thought museums probably already had done this, but I found that although records had been made they were of wax, and most of them had been used so often they were valueless. No proper record of what they were existed."

When the summer of 1931 came around, Wheelwright thought of still another way to pay back Klah for all his hard work. She invited Klah, his nephew Clyde, and the Newcombs to visit her at her home near Northeast Harbor, Maine, a village with a protected waterfront where wealthy city dwellers took refuge from the summer heat of Boston, New York, and Philadelphia. She took her guests rowing and sailing. They visited the Rockefellers, who summered nearby. Klah created one of his sand paintings on the terrace overlooking the ocean.

The sweet memories of early summer did not last. Not long after returning from his long journey, Klah, the medicine man who had seen two oceans, suffered a great loss. His nephew and understudy Beaal Begay became ill and died quite unexpectedly. As if that was not enough of a blow to Klah and Wheelwright, they experienced another misfortune that summer. In the wee hours of the Fourth of July, a gang of thieves descended on Los Luceros under cover of darkness. They broke out a window in the northeast corner of the first floor of the Casa Grande and entered a spare room where luggage and trunks were stored. No one was in the hacienda at the time. Wheelwright was still back East, and the caretaker, Flavio Montoya, and his family were sleeping in the Victorian house.

In a matter of minutes, the thieves made off with many Navajo rugs, artwork, pieces of pawn jewelry, and other valuables. When the break-in was discovered the next morning, Montoya was confident that the culprits were the Night Riders, a ruthless band of criminals that as early as 1924 had operated throughout northern

New Mexico and parts of southern Colorado. These hardened criminals robbed and killed at will. Anyone who reported them for stealing livestock could count on having his barn or home or store burned down.

When Montoya contacted Wheelwright, she was livid, but when she received a complete list of the items stolen from her home, she was relieved. It could have been much worse. The material she and Klah had accumulated was safe, as were many other valuable artifacts and treasures. The exquisite embroidered bedspreads known as colchas that were carefully stored in several large wooden chests were untouched. Even the prized colcha on Wheelwright's own bed was in place.

When local law enforcement appeared to be taking its time investigating the Los Luceros heist, Wheelwright, still at her Maine retreat, joined the chorus of Río Arriba County citizens asking for protection. They all contributed some money—most of it, of course, came from Wheelwright—to hire J. O. Seth, a Santa Fe attorney, and a savvy detective named Bill Martin. Wheelwright later declared that Martin was the "first person who brought law and order into this section of the state." Wheelwright's close friend Alice Corbin Henderson, the Santa Fe poet, acted as coordinator, keeping everyone informed.

Martin wasted no time. He packed his Chevrolet coupe with blankets, food, plenty of ammunition for his six-gun, .30-30 rifle, and shotgun, a half-dozen pairs of handcuffs, and several lengths of chain. He took along a saddle in case he encountered difficult terrain and had to trade his car for a horse.

The manhunt was on. Martin headed for Los Luceros. He interrogated Montoya and pulled a few decent fingerprints from the broken window and doorknobs. He tried to make impressions of some footprints, but the sunbaked ground was too hard. "There was a trail going west toward the Rio Grande, and I followed it for a way and soon saw a number of good horse tracks," Martin wrote many years later in a book he coauthored with Molly Radford Martin, *Bill Martin, American*. "Those led right to a shallow place in the river. I went back to the ranch corral, borrowed a horse, and rode across the river following a trail a very short distance on the other side. Near some trees I spotted a very clear car track in the hard sand, and I made a good paraffin impression of it."

Martin followed the trail but was unable to find any witnesses, so he returned the horse to the corral and drove to the west side of the river. At one of the houses he came upon, Martin found a woman who claimed she had clearly seen the men under a full moon. They had crossed the river on horseback, met another man, and put big sacks into his car. Martin wrote down the descriptions and pressed on for several days but met only people who were afraid to talk. Then he met a man whom the Night Riders had robbed and beaten badly. He was ready to talk. The gang had taken boxes of food from his store. They stole all his sheep and shot his dogs. Then they burned down his hay barn and killed his little daughter's pet lamb. The man knew where the outlaws had gone, and he directed Martin to their camp.

Martin followed a trail of discarded tin cans and came upon two sleeping men. He leveled his rifle and got the jump on them. The dazed outlaws were soon in handcuffs and marched to Martin's car. "There I handcuffed them to the brackets under my dash board and started for Santa Fe," Martin recalled.

Eventually, Martin tracked down and captured more members of the Night Riders, including the leader, Bill McKinley, a cowboy whom Wheelwright knew from her stays at the San Gabriel Ranch. "Big Bill" also had worked for her at Los Luceros and was well acquainted with the property. One of the gang members told Martin that McKinley wanted to rob Wheelwright because she had fired him and, as he put it, "beat him out of some money."

Much of the Los Luceros loot was recovered from trading posts and individual buyers in New Mexico and Colorado. A large cache of rugs, blankets, jewelry, lamps, silverware, and other valuables was unearthed in a chest buried in a cornfield. A Santa Fe judge accepted the Night Riders' guilty pleas and meted out punishment. All of them were sent to the state penitentiary. McKinley received a sentence of six to thirty years. He served five years and was released. But as one newspaper happily reported, "the night riders were no more."

In the wake of the robbery and the sudden death of Klah's understudy, Wheelwright became concerned about the future of her collection and the preservation of Navajo rituals and ceremonial arts. After returning to Los Luceros in the autumn of 1931, she discussed the situation with Klah. He wholeheartedly approved of the plan to create a safe haven for all the recordings, copies of sand paintings, and ceremonial accoutrements. Wheelwright sought the advice of her trusted Santa Fe attorney, J. O. Seth, who was direct and to the point when he told her, "If something happened to you, someone would probably be willing to publish that material, but you are the only person who knows how it should be preserved." Others close to Wheelwright agreed that a repository was essential for the sake of future generations.

An ardent supporter of Wheelwright's plan to build a museum was her Maine neighbor John D. Rockefeller Jr. Rockefeller and she had become acquainted

Steinway & Sons piano in Grand Sala, Casa Grande

during their summers on the Maine coast and had spent time together at San Gabriel Ranch. In the summer of 1930, Rockefeller and his family spent an entire month at Carol Pflaffles' Canjilon Camp. After several visits to Los Luceros, Rockefeller was surprised that someone with Wheelwright's musical prowess did not have a piano in her home. To remedy the situation, Rockefeller gave Wheelwright a Steinway concert grand piano. It was shipped from Denver and uncrated in the west yard. Several ranch hands, mindful that their employment was at stake, carefully hoisted the thousand-pound instrument with heavy-duty block and tackle to the second floor and a place of honor in the sala.

Rockefeller knew of Wheelwright's commitment to historic and cultural preservation. When told of her plan to build a museum, he urged her to proceed. He had observed firsthand Wheelwright's involvement with the Abbe Museum, opened in 1928 as the first institution in Maine to sponsor archaeological research. An early supporter of the Abbe, Rockefeller was grateful when, in 1931, Wheelwright, whose desire to save Indian art and artifacts extended far beyond the Navajo tribe, gave the museum an impressive collection of sixty-two of the finest and oldest examples of Maine Indian basketry. She later served as a museum trustee for five years and continued to be an important donor to the Abbe's ethnographic collections.

In 1927, Rockefeller became the main financial supporter for the establishment of the Laboratory of Anthropology to be built in Santa Fe. Two wealthy New York sisters, Amelia Elizabeth White and Martha Root White, donated fifty acres of their estate on the southeast edge of town for the building site.

In the early 1930s, during the planning phase for the proposed laboratory, Wheelwright approached the newly formed board of directors and asked them to consider acquiring the vast collection she and Klah had assembled over the years. At first, the board members were open to the proposal, but that quickly changed when Wheelwright made it clear she had one nonnegotiable condition that had to be met. Both Wheelwright and Klah insisted, out of respect for Navajo people and the sacred objects, that the building be designed in the shape of a traditional octagonal hogan. Wheelwright wanted her friend William Penhallow Henderson to design what she called the Navajo House of Prayer. "It is difficult to think of sand-paintings without the hogan—just as it is impossible to think of a Catholic Mass without the Cathedral," Henderson was quoted as saying in the Wheelwright Museum of the American Indian National Register of Historic Places Registration Form.

The board's building committee rejected Wheelwright's plan. They decided the hogan-shaped structure was totally incompatible with what they envisioned: the popular Santa Fe style, Pueblo Revival architecture that had become so trendy throughout the town. The board further objected because, in their words, a museum "conceived upon an emotional, rather than a scientific basis" was contrary to the purposes of the Laboratory of Anthropology. The plan of John Gaw Meem, the leading architect of Pueblo Revival style, was chosen for the laboratory.

"I disagreed because I felt it was not fitting that a museum of the Navaho religion should be housed in a Spanish-American building," Wheelwright wrote in her autobiography. "My original plan was that the Navaho Museum should be part of the Laboratory of Anthropology, and I offered to maintain it for ten years under those conditions, but when I found that no one on the committee could understand my point of view I withdrew my offer and decided to initiate a separate organization."

In 1935, much to the displeasure of the mostly male anthropologists at the laboratory, Amelia White gave Wheelwright some land adjacent to the Laboratory of Anthropology to build what eventually was named the Museum of Navajo Ceremonial Art. Wheelwright picked Henderson as project architect. Klah was a consultant, and Alice Corbin Henderson became the museum's first curator. In 1936, Klah conducted a traditional House Blessing ceremony at the museum groundbreaking, but he did not take part in the formal opening a year later.

In February 1937, when influenza swept across the Navajo reservation, Klah was stricken with pneumonia while caring for sick family and friends. He died at the hospital in Gallup and was laid to rest at the Navajo settlement of Tohatchi, New Mexico. Later, his body was reinterred on the grounds of the museum he had helped to create. A relative of Klah's named Big Man was asked to give the blessing. He came by bus, accompanied by most of Klah's family, and blessed the building by praying and touching the four cardinal points with pollen.

7   Maria Chabot

IN LATE 1934, MARIA CHABOT, a fresh-faced, twenty-one-year-old Texan in braids, made her way north from Santa Fe in a borrowed Model T Ford to visit Los Luceros. Toting her Brownie camera, she was met by the housekeeper at the front door of the Casa Grande and taken up the steep wooden stairs to the grand sala where Mary Cabot Wheelwright waited.

Chabot was working as a part-time photographer for a state vocational training program managed by Brice H. Sewell, an industrial sculptor and director of Spanish handicrafts at the University of New Mexico. Her assignment was to create a photographic and written record of Spanish Colonial folk art. She stopped at Los Luceros to photograph Wheelwright's sizable collection of Hispano furniture, textiles, woven rugs and blankets, embroidered colchas, and religious objects hand-carved by artisans in the villages of northern New Mexico.

After a full day of work at Los Luceros, pausing only for lunch in the downstairs dining room and later for sips of Wheelwright's mandatory midafternoon tea, Chabot calculated she would need several more sessions to photograph the collection properly. In the course of those visits, she developed a friendship with the woman who would become her benefactor. It was the start of a mercurial relationship that would last for almost twenty-five years.

Wheelwright, more than twice Chabot's age, had little in common with Chabot, who came from a reasonably well-to-do family in San Antonio, Texas. Chabot's paternal grandfather, George Stooks Chabot, had served as the British

Unknown photographer.
*Maria Chabot at Los Luceros
on horseback*, undated.
Maria Chabot Papers,
1866–2002, undated. Georgia
O'Keeffe Museum. Gift of
Maria Chabot [2013.3.1].

consul to Mexico during the turbulent 1860s when the Republic of Mexico
fought for its survival against a French invasion and subsequent occupation. Her
grandmother, Mary Van Derlip Chabot, a native of Gonzales, Texas, site of the first
military engagement of the Texas Revolution, was a proper Victorian lady and an
accomplished landscape and portrait artist.

By 1873, the Chabot family had established themselves in San Antonio.
George Stooks Chabot became a highly successful commission merchant deal-
ing in wool, hides, and cotton. The Chabots' two-story stone house on Madison
Street, built in 1876, remains a San Antonio landmark.

Maria Chabot was born there in 1913. Her given name was Mary Lea, but
for most of her life she went by Maria. Her father, Charles Jasper Chabot, was the
younger of two sons. Her mother, Olive Anderson Johnson Chabot, was his third
wife. Both had children from earlier marriages.

A good student with an insatiable curiosity, Maria demonstrated a true talent
when it came to writing and the arts. She credited Ella Butler, her high school
English teacher, with instilling in her a love of great literature. The two of them

stayed in touch until Butler's death in San Antonio in 1946. "I filled the Rio Grande with my tears," Chabot wrote about her grief for her teacher in a January 1947 letter. Although she excelled in high school, Chabot did not go on to college. She was impatient to make her way in the world. After graduation, she took a job writing advertising copy for one of San Antonio's largest department stores.

By 1933, she was ready to move on and see more of the world. That spring, Chabot quit her job and traveled to Mexico, accompanied by her friend Rudolf Staffel, a young painter who had studied at the Chicago Art Institute and would become a world-famous ceramic artist. While in Mexico, they stayed with one of Chabot's relatives, Emily Edwards, a celebrated painter and an art historian who helped to establish the San Antonio Conservation Society, an architectural and cultural preservation organization.

Devoting much of her time to writing and painting, Chabot blossomed in Mexico. Edwards was a gracious hostess and a superb teacher and guide. She introduced Chabot to Santa Fe artists and art patrons, and intellectuals who frequently spent time in Mexico City. Soon Chabot became friends with Wheelwright's friends, fresco painter Olive Rush, writer Erna Fergusson, and Dorothy Stewart, an influential Santa Fe printmaker and artist. Stewart and her older sister, Margretta Stewart Dietrich, were the daughters of a prominent Philadelphia physician. The sisters became entranced with New Mexico during a 1925 visit, and two years later they moved to Santa Fe.

By befriending this impressive collection of women, Chabot had an opportunity to meet some of Mexico's leading painters—Diego Rivera and his wife, Frida Kahlo, José Clemente Orozco, and Rufino Tamayo.

At some point early on during her time in Mexico, Chabot began an intimate relationship with Dorothy Stewart. They would periodically live together for the next several years and remain close friends for many more. In October 1933, the two women went by ship from Mexico to New York. During the eight months Chabot spent in New York, she had no luck finding a day job as a copywriter to support her literary efforts. Fortunately, Stewart provided help with expenses.

It was through Stewart that Chabot became acquainted with a variety of artists either residing in or visiting New York. One of the visitors she met was Taos painter Dorothy Brett, an aristocratic Englishwoman who preferred the bohemian life of an artist and came to America with D. H. and Frieda Lawrence. When Chabot met her, Brett was in the midst of producing her series of paintings of the renowned conductor Leopold Stokowski. During a visit to Taos, the maestro had made quite an impression on Brett. When she received "two very lovely letters" from the "very lovely man," she dashed off to New York and Philadelphia to sketch him while he conducted. Thus the series of sixteen paintings called *The Stokowski Symphony* was created.

At about the time that Chabot met Brett, she also was introduced to Alfred Stieglitz—photography pioneer, modern art promoter, and husband of the emerging painter Georgia O'Keeffe. He owned and operated the gallery where Brett wanted to display her Stokowski paintings. Brett tried twice but failed to convince Stieglitz to exhibit them.

Chabot was exhilarated by the swirl of activity and exposure to the artistic lifestyle. She wanted more. In early 1935, she accompanied Stewart to Hanover, New Hampshire, to call on Orozco, just up from Mexico to complete his monumental fresco cycle, *The Epic of American Civilization*, in the Baker Library at Dartmouth College. Standing before the almost finished mural, Chabot was in awe of the twenty-four fresco panels. She was so inspired, she began to write short stories and submitted several for publication before returning to San Antonio to check on her parents. Although none of her stories was accepted, she continued to write. She was anxious to keep on the move. After only a month in Texas, she returned to New Mexico. Chabot had become a committed nomad. "I was off on a cultural binge all my life," Chabot said in 1992, quoted by Sharon Niederman in the *Santa Fe Reporter.*

She arrived in Santa Fe in May 1934 at the invitation of Dorothy Stewart and her sister, Margretta Dietrich. For the next year, while Dietrich traveled to China, Chabot lived with Stewart in Dietrich's historic Canyon Road adobe residence, known as the Juan José Prada House.

Stewart constructed a large studio in another nearby historic building that her sister owned on Canyon Road, a long, winding artery that remained unpaved until the mid-1960s. The original old adobe had been expanded into a long one-story hacienda in the mid-nineteenth century by James Johnson, one of the most prosperous wholesale and retail merchants in the days of the Santa Fe Trail. The sisters named it El Zaguán (The Passageway) because of the long passage through the building that led to a Victorian garden bordered by a white picket fence and shaded by a pair of stately horse chestnut trees. The trees were landmarks on Canyon Road for many years. Other rooms were converted to apartments for other artists and writers. Farther east on Canyon Road, Dietrich purchased another notable property, built in 1756, known as the Rafael Borrego House. She thus saved three historically significant structures from redevelopment.

In the summer of 1934, comfortably ensconced with Stewart on Canyon Road, Chabot started the part-time job that brought her to Los Luceros and the start of her relationship with Wheelwright. After an interlude of travel, Chabot was back in Santa Fe by January 1936, living with Stewart and Dietrich on Canyon Road.

In addition to her efforts to save and preserve Santa Fe's architectural and cultural landmarks, Dietrich, like her friend Mary Wheelwright, devoted much of her time to advocacy for the Pueblo and Navajo people. Deitrich served for twenty-one years as chair of the New Mexico Association on Indian Affairs (NMAIA), a volunteer organization founded in 1922 to lobby against legislation detrimental to Pueblo people and their lands. Wheelwright was a board member. Twelve years later, the NMAIA joined forces with the Southwestern Indian Fair Committee, formed by Dr. Edgar Lee Hewett, director of both the Museum of New Mexico and the School of American Research. Their goal was to create and promote a market for the arts and crafts of the pueblos.

Dietrich knew the best way to accomplish this mission was to reach a wide audience beyond New Mexico. She recruited Chabot as her assistant and turned her loose. Eager to have her writing published, Chabot produced a series of articles for *New Mexico Magazine* touting Indian pottery, weaving, and other crafts. Based on her observations of the crowded outdoor markets in Mexican villages, Chabot convinced Dietrich and the other members of the association that the Indian fairs should not be held indoors, but outside, beneath the Palace of the Governor's portal on the Santa Fe Plaza. Thanks to Chabot, the Indian vendors set their own prices and sell directly to the public, according to author Bruce Bernstein.

The seasonal Indian markets continued through 1939 with great success and eventually became daily markets when the Museum of New Mexico sponsored the Native American Vendors Program, which continues to protect the Pueblo artists and ensure the authenticity of their work. The hard work and vision of Chabot and her fellow advocates also set the stage for the annual Santa Fe Indian Market, which has become the largest and most important Native American arts event in the nation.

As a reward for her hard work and to appease her chronic wanderlust, Chabot spent 1937 and part of 1938 traveling abroad with Dorothy Stewart. Once Chabot was back in Santa Fe, she continued to support the restructuring of the Indian arts and crafts markets and resumed working on a Works Progress Administration (WPA) project that focused on all matters related to the enhancement of tribal art. Always ready to take on more work, often to her detriment, Chabot decided to fulfill her dream of launching a periodical devoted to not only American Indian art but also indigenous arts of the world. She needed to find a funding source and a publisher—a formidable task in the midst of the Great Depression.

Besides finding local support in Santa Fe, Chabot knew she had to look beyond New Mexico for financial backing. To that end, she sought encouragement and advice from a woman she had first met five years earlier, Mary Cabot Wheelwright.

Chabot temporarily moved to New York, where she devoted three months to promoting her magazine and looking for money to finance its publication. While Chabot was in New York, she was invited to Wheelwright's summer home on Sutton Island, Maine. Wheelwright was supportive of Chabot's plans and impressed by the young woman's high energy and interest in American Indian art. Likely as a result of Wheelwright's connections, Chabot landed interview appointments with three of the largest philanthropic organizations in the nation, the Rockefeller, Guggenheim, and Carnegie foundations.

During Chabot's visit to Maine, Wheelwright introduced her to Abby Rockefeller, a neighbor and close friend who was a major supporter of the arts and a driving force in the establishment of the Museum of Modern Art (MOMA) in New York. Although she was a member of an incredibly wealthy family, she did not possess great personal wealth herself, and her husband, John D. Rockefeller Jr., was not a fan of modern art. Consequently, the funding for the museum came from Mrs. Rockefeller's dogged solicitation of major corporate donors and prominent New Yorkers.

Chabot's visit with Mrs. Rockefeller went well. She was impressed by Chabot's pitch for the establishment of the magazine. Later, when talk turned to MOMA's plans to present a major show of American Indian art, Chabot suggested some imaginative display options. Mrs. Rockefeller was so excited by the prospects that she set up a meeting in Vermont between Wheelwright and Chabot and art historian Alfred H. Barr Jr., founding director of MOMA and one of the most influential forces in the modern art movement. The meeting with Barr was cordial, but nothing came of it for Chabot. None of the foundations awarded her any funding for the proposed magazine, nor was she given a role in the big *Indian Art of the United States* exhibition that drew huge crowds to MOMA in 1941. It was organized by two important figures from the art world, Frederick Huntington Douglas, curator of Indian art at the Denver Art Museum, and René d'Harnoncourt, general manager of the federal Indian Arts and Crafts Board.

Discouraged by the rejection, Chabot returned to Santa Fe and snapped up a temporary job with the New Mexico Association on Indian Affairs that required her to spend time on the vast Navajo reservation. Her assignment was to uncover any problems experienced by the Navajos, investigate their complaints, and write a detailed report.

After two months of traversing the reservation, she was ready to draft her report. Instead of returning to Santa Fe, however, Chabot accepted an invitation sent from Wheelwright back East to stay at Los Luceros. In the early autumn, Cabot was just finishing her report, entitled "Urgent Navajo Problems: Observations and Recommendations Based on a Recent Study by the New Mexico Association on Indian Affairs," when Wheelwright arrived at the ranch for one of her periodic visits.

Wheelwright was in the throes of putting together a book about the creation story of the Navajo people as told by her late friend Hosteen Klah. She enlisted Chabot to stay on at Los Luceros to help with the manuscript and to sort and classify an assortment of objects that Wheelwright had collected during trips to China, India, and Tibet.

The publication of the book was very important to Wheelwright. It contained transcribed ceremonial songs and chants, along with Klah's explanation of the Navajo creation story. The book, *Navajo Creation Myth: The Story of Emergence*, and the Wheelwright Museum of the American Indian represented a culmination of the many years Wheelwright and Klah had devoted to ensuring the posterity of Navajo religion and culture.

Keenly aware of the book's significance, Chabot was proud of her contributions, and Wheelwright was forever grateful for her help. They liked each other's company and spent a good part of each day together. Except for breakfast, which Wheelwright always ate in the solitude of her bedroom, the two of them shared most of their meals, enjoyed horseback rides across the pastures and the pueblo lands, and looked forward to afternoon tea discussions of art, philosophy, literature, and, of course, their shared love of all things American Indian.

Chabot was in no particular hurry to leave Los Luceros. It was a comfortable abode and conducive to her creative urges. She made time for writing, perused the library, and pitched in with some of the daily chores. If she found herself getting bored, a quick trip to Santa Fe for a visit with friends was the best remedy.

Then Chabot felt the inevitable itch. By the time the cottonwood leaves started to turn colors, she was ready to take on a new project. Opportunity soon came calling. It would influence the rest of Chabot's life and have a direct impact on the future of Los Luceros.

Following spread: Apple blossoms in orchard in spring

Baby farm animals: day-old lamb, newborn lamb, rooster, donkey, newborn calf romping in pasture, and day-old calf

Opposite: Mowing alfalfa in summer

Following spread: Barnyard

Previous spread, above, and opposite: Chabot House

8   The Lucky Stars

On a golden October afternoon in 1940, Mary Cabot Wheelwright, Maria Chabot, and Georgia O'Keeffe sat down for lunch in the sunlit dining room of the Casa Grande at Los Luceros. Although none of them knew it at the time, all the lucky stars fell into place at that luncheon, which brought together three women who each in her own way ensured the future of Los Luceros for decades to come. Wheelwright had already invested seventeen years of her life resurrecting and rehabilitating the historic property and would continue to do so for many more years. Chabot would one day take over the daily management of Los Luceros, and O'Keeffe's influence resulted from her recruitment of future owners Charles and Nina Collier.

Wheelwright and O'Keeffe were already well acquainted. They had met years before and frequently visited at art events and social gatherings in New Mexico and New York. Two O'Keeffe paintings—*Abstraction*, 1930, and *Pedernal, New Mexico*, 1936—graced the wall next to Wheelwright's bed at Los Luceros. Chabot also admired O'Keeffe and found herself drawn to her paintings. During one of her visits to New York, Chabot had met Alfred Stieglitz but not O'Keeffe. The Los Luceros luncheon was her first face-to-face encounter with the illustrious artist.

Twenty-seven-year-old Chabot and fifty-three-year-old O'Keeffe instantly connected. Years later, O'Keeffe fondly recalled that day at Los Luceros when she first met "a tall handsome young woman" who appeared bright and energetic with a deep appreciation of nature. Soon after the luncheon at Los Luceros, O'Keeffe invited Wheelwright and Chabot for tea at her Ghost Ranch summer home. Chabot was completely entranced by the setting and magnificent vistas of the Ghost Ranch property. It was obvious that O'Keeffe felt the same; Ghost Ranch was her heaven on earth. In 1940, she still devoted much of her time to Stieglitz in New York, but her creative spirit soared during her summers in northern New Mexico.

For most of the 1920s, O'Keeffe lived and worked in New York with Alfred Stieglitz, whom she had married in 1924. They lived in Manhattan and spent the summer months at the Stieglitz family's retreat on the western shoreline of Lake George in the Adirondack Mountains, where O'Keeffe created many of her best landscape paintings. Stieglitz became her biggest supporter and promoter. He staged many exhibitions of her work and was diligent in determining whether a potential buyer was worthy of owning an O'Keeffe.

Considered by many to be one of the greatest creative partnerships in American art history, their relationship was not without its share of problems and challenges. As Stieglitz grew older, he developed a serious heart condition. Twenty-two years O'Keeffe's senior, he frequently complained of feeling ill. Then there were the whispers of infidelities. Rumors abounded but for the most part were never substantiated that both O'Keeffe and Stieglitz had their share of romantic dalliances outside their marriage. But in 1927, Stieglitz began a very public love affair with Dorothy Norman, a twenty-one-year-old heiress.

O'Keeffe, weary of nursing an ailing husband and unhappy about his infidelity, was restless and depressed and needed a change of place. In the frigid New York winter of 1928, she found at least a temporary remedy for her distress. That winter, Taos artist Dorothy Brett traveled to New York for an extended visit. She stayed at the Shelton, the hotel where Alfred Stieglitz and Georgia O'Keeffe lived. Brett and O'Keeffe were fond of each other. Both women looked forward to their frequent meetings for breakfast in the hotel cafeteria. Brett's lingering memory of O'Keeffe was her distinctive profile and her "strong white hands touching and lifting everything, even the boiled eggs, as if they were living things."

In private conversations, Brett told O'Keeffe about her life in Taos and the beauty and allure of northern New Mexico. O'Keeffe was enchanted by all she heard and recalled her brief but memorable earlier visit to New Mexico with her sister in 1917. She began to think that perhaps a return to the Southwest was in order.

That same winter, Mabel Dodge Luhan also visited New York with her husband, Tony Lujan. (Mabel spelled her married name Luhan instead of Lujan so that her East Coast friends would know how to pronounce it.) During their stay, the Lujans spent considerable time with O'Keeffe at the Shelton and at Mabel

Luhan's apartment at One Fifth Avenue, a new residential Art Deco skyscraper a block from Washington Square Park and Greenwich Village. Just as Brett had done, Mabel Luhan, always anxious to lure more artists and writers to Taos, painted a verbal picture of New Mexico that O'Keeffe found irresistible. When Luhan offered her lodging and a studio, the seduction was complete. O'Keeffe's mind was made up.

On April 27, 1929, O'Keeffe bid Stieglitz good-bye and boarded a train to New Mexico, accompanied by her friend Rebecca Strand. After three days on the train watching the passing landscape and sky open up wider and wider, O'Keeffe was eager to launch her working holiday. Once she arrived, she knew that her life would never be the same.

After making the rounds of Santa Fe, O'Keeffe and Strand bought seats on a Fred Harvey Indian Detour motor coach headed west on Route 66 to the annual green corn dance at San Felipe Pueblo. They planned to proceed to Taos and surprise Mabel Luhan by showing up unannounced at her door. That plan was quickly scuttled when O'Keeffe and Strand arrived at San Felipe and immediately bumped into Mabel and Tony, who had also come to see the dance. That evening, all of them returned to Santa Fe and left the next morning for Taos.

For the next four months, O'Keeffe and Strand lived and worked at the Lujan's Los Gallos. They stayed in one of the guestrooms in the three-story adobe Big House for three weeks and then moved to the more private Casa Rosita, the Pink House. They also were provided with separate studio space. O'Keeffe was ecstatic and immediately recognized that New Mexico was where she belonged. "I am West again and it is as fine as I remembered it—maybe finer," O'Keeffe explained in a letter to her sister Catherine Klenert. "There is nothing to say about it except the fact that for me it is the only place."

For several weeks, O'Keeffe and Strand saw little of their hostess. Less than a week after arriving in Taos, O'Keeffe was busily painting. She was drawn to both architecture and nature. Her subjects included Taos Pueblo and the San Francisco de Assisi Mission Church at Rancho de Taos. While staying with Brett twenty miles north of Taos at Kiowa Ranch, where D. H. Lawrence had lived, O'Keeffe became interested in a towering ponderosa pine. When he was at the ranch, Lawrence often had sat on a carpenter's bench beneath the tree to write. "I used to lie on the bench and look up, and eventually there was nothing to do but paint the tree," recalled O'Keeffe in Roxana Robinson's *Georgia O'Keeffe: A Life* when asked about *The Lawrence Tree*, one of her favorite paintings.

Another source of creative stimulation was the wide circle of artists, writers, poets, photographers, and intellectuals whom Luhan enticed to Taos. O'Keeffe forged a lifetime friendship with a young photographer fifteen years her junior named Ansel Adams. The dinner conversations and evening gatherings brought together a mix of colorful guests such as journalist Willard "Spud" Johnson, Santa Fe poet Witter Bynner, and artists John Marin, Cady Wells, and Andrew Dasburg.

Among the many people O'Keeffe met at Los Gallos that busy summer of 1929 was twenty-year-old Charles Wood Collier. That initial encounter between the middle-aged artist and the young college student developed into a cherished friendship for both of them. It also proved to have a lasting impact on Los Luceros when, thirty years later, O'Keeffe convinced Collier to purchase the historic property. To appreciate Charles Collier's role in the story of Los Luceros, it is important to understand the Collier family's lasting influence on New Mexico.

Charles was the oldest son of John Collier (1884–1968), a remarkable visionary and social activist destined to achieve national acclaim as a progressive reformer championing the rights of Pueblo Indians. John's parents, who both came from well-regarded Georgia families, died when their sons were still young. In an attempt to recover from the loss, John Collier spent the entire summer of 1901 camping alone in the wilderness of the southern Appalachian Mountains. During that time, he made the decision to reject all desire for worldly success. He concluded that his inheritance would be best used preparing him for a life of service to others. After graduating as valedictorian of his high school class, he set out to do so in New York.

As an undergraduate at Columbia University, Collier was exposed to the latest trends in literature, philosophy, and politics and met many of the most articulate writers and teachers of the early twentieth century. Those early years in New York allowed Collier to form beliefs that guided him throughout his life. Working in an emigrant settlement house showed him the value of ethnic and cultural diversity.

After college, Collier returned to Georgia and held jobs as a social worker and then as a reporter. He traveled to Paris to study psychology, and on the steamer voyage to France, he met Lucy Wood, whom he married in 1906. After a honeymoon in Europe, John and Lucy Collier returned to America in 1907. They went no farther than New York, where Collier accepted a position as a community organizer with the People's Institute.

Although for more than a decade Collier spent most of his time in the boroughs of New York, he and Lucy made their home about twenty miles northwest of Manhattan in the Rockland County hamlet of Sparkill. All three of their sons, Charles, Donald, and John Jr., were born there.

While adjusting to fatherhood and balancing parental duties with his work at the institute, Collier became closely involved with the intellectual and bohemian scene that thrived in Greenwich Village. He attended the evening salons that Mabel Dodge hosted weekly in her elegant brownstone apartment at 23 Fifth Avenue on the corner of Ninth Street. There, artists, authors, socialists, Bolsheviks, anarchists, and all stripes of the intellectually curious met to discuss and debate gender equality, avant-garde ideas in art, the virtues of free love, political and economic reform, the merits of socialism, birth-control education, the contradictions of capitalism, and other issues of the day. Among the other visitors were Isadora Duncan, Emma Goldman, Andrew Dasburg, Amy Lowell, Upton Sinclair, Ida Rauh, John Reed, Max Eastman, Louise Bryant, John Sloan, Margaret Sanger, and Carl Van Vechten.

When the armistice ended World War I in 1918, the Colliers, like most of their friends and associates, knew major change was in store for not only the nation but also the world. In New York City, public and private funding and political support dried up for Collier's various reform programs. In 1919, he resigned from the People's Institute and moved his family across the country to Mill Valley, California, just north of San Francisco. Collier signed a one-year contract to act as director of the California State Housing and Immigration Commission's adult education program called Americanization.

The timing could not have been worse. Across the nation, in the wake of the so-called Great War and the Bolshevik Revolution in Russia, fervent patriotism turned into an irrational fear of a Communist-inspired revolution on American soil. After delivering a speech in which he praised the Bolshevik Revolution, Collier was placed under surveillance by the agency that became the FBI for what were considered his "communistic beliefs." As a result, the funding for his Americanization program was slashed to the bone.

A disillusioned Collier tendered his resignation and considered the best options for himself and his family. Ever since his friend Mabel Dodge had discovered New Mexico in 1917 and moved to Taos, she had repeatedly invited the Colliers and other old friends from her Greenwich Village salon to visit her. Now was the time. Before long, the Colliers found themselves on their way to Taos. It proved to be a significant detour.

The Colliers arrived at Taos in a blinding snowstorm on Christmas Eve 1920. Mabel and Tony Lujan greeted them with mugs of hot chocolate for the boys and brandies for John and Lucy. Before they could unpack, all of them hurried to Taos Pueblo for the Christmas Eve procession and ceremonies. That night at Los Gallos, the Colliers were the first guests to stay in what Mabel called the Two-Story House, a newly built adobe with six rooms and a second-story balcony.

Three days later, they returned to Taos Pueblo for the Deer Dance. The resonant pulsing of the big drums sounded like a giant's beating heart. Everyone stood transfixed by the dancers wearing deerhide capes and antlered heads as they moved through the shadows and sweet smoke of the fires. Even the Collier boys, young as they were, realized that they were witnessing something special. Their father was mesmerized by what he saw at Taos and remained so the rest of his life.

The epiphany Collier experienced in Taos had a profound and lasting effect on him and consequently on his entire family. Collier spent much of the next year in New Mexico immersing himself in the history and culture of American Indian tribes, especially the Pueblo people. At long last, he found what he had been searching for since he was a young man. He was convinced that Pueblo culture provided a fitting model for the rest of the nation because it did not focus on the material aspects of life.

Back in California in 1921, Collier had become the research agent for the Indian Welfare Committee, a division of the General Federation of Women's Clubs concerned with forced assimilation of tribal people. He gained national attention that year through his leadership role in opposing the ill-advised Bursum Bill, which would have resulted in New Mexico pueblos losing tens of thousands of acres of ancestral lands guaranteed by treaties. Collier not only mobilized public opinion nationwide but also mobilized the pueblos. He accompanied a Pueblo delegation to Washington to testify before Congress and explain the adverse effects of the proposed legislation on the pueblos. The Bursum Bill went down to defeat. Flushed with victory, Collier founded the American Indian Defense Association to fight for protection of the property and religious freedom of all Indians.

Throughout the 1920s, the Collier family spent a considerable amount of time in New Mexico, mostly staying with the Lujans in Taos. All three boys took to New Mexico from the start. They eavesdropped on the conversations of Mabel Luhan's interesting adult guests, made regular pilgrimages to Kit Carson's grave in the nearby cemetery, and expressed great delight when their father allowed one of them to tag along on visits to the pueblos.

Of the three sons, it was clear that the youngest, John Jr., required extra care. He was eight years old when he was struck by an automobile not far from home in Mill Valley. Despite the accident, John Collier Jr. developed into a bright and capable man. In New Mexico, he spent much of his time staying with mentors he found at Taos Pueblo and received informal instruction in painting from the Taos artist Nicolai Fechin. In San Francisco, when he was just twelve years old, John Jr.

John Collier Sr. and sons at Los Luceros, ca. 1960s. *Left to right*: John Collier Sr., John Collier Jr., Charles Collier, and Donald Collier. Courtesy of Lucy Collier.

apprenticed himself to the painter Maynard Dixon, who was then married to photographer Dorothea Lange. John Collier Jr. would go on to become a renowned photographer as well as a leader in visual and applied anthropology.

It was obvious when he was a boy that Donald Collier, the middle son, was destined to become a scholar. He credited his professional success to an upbringing in the constant company of brilliant minds and his early exposure to anthropology and archaeology in New Mexico and Arizona. He graduated from the University of California at Berkeley and received his doctorate in anthropology from the University of Chicago. From the time he was a boy until his death, Donald Collier was concerned with the issue of American Indians. A longtime curator at the Field Museum of Natural History in Chicago and a leader in the study of North and South American Indians, he was particularly concerned with the respectful and proper exhibition of their personal artifacts.

Charles Wood Collier, the eldest of the sons, was the wild card. He could be unpredictable. His father found him puzzling, a riddle to be solved. Perhaps that is why John Collier most often picked the inscrutable Charles to escort him as he made the rounds of pueblos and villages throughout the 1920s. Charles Collier cherished the memories of those times. With his father, he climbed a ladder at Taos Pueblo and entered a chamber where council members waited. Charles recalled hearing Tony Lujan speak, his voice trembling with rare emotion. The boy went with his father to Santo Domingo and San Juan and to the other pueblos to the west. They sat in rooms packed with delegates from many villages. Some wore boots and some wore beaded moccasins and necklaces of coral and turquoise. The air was thick with smoke from cigarettes made from dried cornhusks and twists of tobacco. Later, they ate lunches of stew, fry bread, and watermelon.

Then, on the way home, they would stop at Los Luceros to visit Mary Cabot Wheelwright and her guests. Charles Collier always remembered the big cotton-woods, the deep flowing acequia, and the Casa Grande. He never forgot those times with his father at the old rancho on the Río Grande.

9   The Convergence

In 1929, Charles Collier did not have a care in the world. College was coming up in the fall, but until then, he was free to roam and take in the important sites of northern New Mexico, including Los Luceros, Alcalde, and the environs. That summer, at Mabel Dodge Luhan's Taos compound, he stopped at Los Luceros whenever he could borrow his father's motorcar for a sightseeing cruise. Often, Georgia O'Keeffe went along on the ride.

O'Keeffe and her roommate, Beck Strand, purchased a black Ford sedan for $678 and promptly named it Hello. Tony Lujan and then Beck attempted to teach Georgia how to drive until Charles Collier took over and became O'Keeffe's unofficial squire. Near the end of summer, Charles and Georgia joined some friends who had a Rolls-Royce and a Packard and drove to the Grand Canyon, with frequent stops along the way.

When she returned to New York, O'Keeffe left her Ford in Taos, where Dorothy Brett sold it for her. Back in the city, O'Keeffe was pleased that Charles Collier contacted her as soon as he arrived in New York to study architecture at Columbia University. O'Keeffe and Stieglitz made sure young Collier was on the invitation lists to all the best gallery openings and lectures and had tickets for Broadway shows and the complete cycle of Wagner's *Ring* at the New York Metropolitan Opera. Collier was such a frequent dinner guest that the doormen at the Shelton greeted him by name.

In the spring of 1930, O'Keeffe decided to get another automobile. She bought a new Ford that looked like Hello and then fretted for weeks because, unlike New Mexico, New York State required every operator of a motor vehicle to have a driver's license. After many sleepless nights, she took the driving test and passed. She was relieved but still concerned because she had never really driven in traffic, only on empty roads in New Mexico.

"Am driving ten miles every day to the nearest uncomfortable town with our favorite taxi man during the busiest hours and I drive up and down the main street—around corners—turn around," O'Keeffe wrote Brett from Lake George, as quoted by Nancy Hopkin Reily in *Georgia O'Keeffe*. "When I wake up in the night—a feeling of gloom comes over me and I decide to sell my second Ford— In the morning my stubbornness starts me off driving again—and in the dark hours of the night I despair again—That is the way I am—Driving a bit in the little town here will make N.Y. much easier, and if I am going to drive at all I want to be able to drive anywhere."

Then, from out of nowhere, like a knight in shining armor, Charles Collier showed up from Taos to spend two weeks with O'Keeffe and Stieglitz. Driving lessons resumed for O'Keeffe. Stieglitz was so pleased that he made three striking photographic portraits of Collier and personally mounted the gelatin silver prints to tissue and dry-mounted them to boards.

During Collier's visit, O'Keeffe decided a long road trip was in order. She "had a fever," as she put it, to go to the seaside resort town of York, Maine, and wanted Collier and Stieglitz to join her, according to correspondence in the Lucy Collier Collection. Young Collier was the chauffeur for the trip. During the four-day drive to the Maine coast, Stieglitz regaled Collier with stories from his younger days, including one about the illegitimate daughter he had fathered as the result of an illicit affair with a German countess.

At York, they checked in at a seaside guesthouse on Long Sands Beach, where O'Keeffe had stayed on earlier visits. Every morning, they walked past a cranberry bog to a boardwalk that led to the edge of the Atlantic. They scavenged the wide beach for seashells and driftwood and the odd bits of flotsam and jetsam that became treasures. In the evenings, shore dinners were served at the Wahnita, formerly the Union Bluff House and about to be renamed the York Plaza Hotel. After a feast of chowder, lobster, and littleneck clams, they topped off the evening with saltwater taffy and a band concert in the town park. The glow of a lighthouse showed them the way home to the cottage.

Back at Lake George after the trip to Maine, Collier prepared to return to Taos for the summer break. He drove the Ford from New York to New Mexico. When O'Keeffe came by train, Collier picked her up at the Santa Fe Railway depot at Raton, New Mexico, less than one hundred miles northwest of Taos. In the autumn, Collier drove the auto back to New York and O'Keeffe went home by train, a cycle the two of them followed for three years. Each time, Stieglitz wired Collier money to cover expenses.

O'Keeffe's 1930 visit to Taos was not quite as cordial as in the previous year. Mabel Luhan, put off by what she considered O'Keeffe's flirtatiousness with Tony, allowed her to stay at Los Gallos but arranged for her to take all her meals at a local hotel. Although they remained friends, it would be the last summer O'Keeffe stayed with Luhan.

During the early 1930s, O'Keeffe's friendship with Charles Collier continued to grow. Every summer, she made countless solo excursions throughout northern New Mexico in her Ford, but she also searched for inspiration in the company

Maria Chabot. *Georgia O'Keeffe, Ghost Ranch Patio*, 1944. Letters to Alfred Stieglitz, 1933-1944, undated. Georgia O'Keeffe Museum [MS. OKAS.213p].

of the young man responsible for introducing her to the country where she had found her true home—Ghost Ranch and Abiquiú.

"A friend of mine took me there," O'Keeffe explained in a 1983 interview with Andy Warhol. "He looked at me and said, 'Well, you've traveled over a good deal of this country. But you haven't seen the best part of it yet. I'll take you up and show you the most beautiful part of the country.' That was Charles Collier. So we drove there."

Neither of them forgot that drive. When the Ford sedan wound its way into the southeastern end of the Chama River Valley, O'Keeffe connected to a land that would influence her life and art, creating her lasting identity. It was as serendipitous as the afternoon in 1940 when O'Keeffe and Maria Chabot first met and the stars aligned at Los Luceros, the property that Chabot would one day manage and that Collier first saw as a boy and later owned as a man.

On that summer day in 1934 when Collier and O'Keeffe rode around the high mesas, red cliffs, and colorful landscape that would inspire some of O'Keeffe's most famous works of art, they could not find the road through the badlands to Ghost Ranch. Soon after, however, O'Keeffe nosed around and learned there was no sign marking the ranch gate, only a steer skull. She immediately took off and drove directly to Ghost Ranch.

When O'Keeffe inquired about getting a room, she was told that all the adobe casitas were booked for the summer, but on the following day, there was a room open for just a single night. O'Keeffe booked it. She returned to Alcalde, gathered up her belongings and art supplies, and was back early the next morning. Then a family canceled their reservation because of illness, allowing O'Keeffe to spend the entire summer at Ghost Ranch.

In 1934, Ghost Ranch remained under the ownership of Carol Stanley, who had resumed using her maiden name after divorcing Roy Pfaffle a few years before. Their once popular San Gabriel Ranch in Alcalde, where many well-known guests had stayed, including Mary Cabot Wheelwright and the Rockefellers, was severely impacted by the crash of 1929 and the economic depression that followed. There were fewer and fewer guests, and Pfaffle, already a serious drinker, increased his consumption of alcohol to the point that he was useless to Carol as both a business partner and a husband. During the winter months, Carol brought in some income by giving piano lessons, but it was not enough. The Pfaffles were bankrupt.

Financial backers of the San Gabriel Ranch prepared to divide up the land. In July 1931, Carol ended her marriage and abandoned San Gabriel Ranch. The shareholders, including Wheelwright and members of Roy Pfaffle's family, fore-closed on the property. As a result, Wheelwright added to her Los Luceros hold-ings another 132 acres of land that had been held by the Pfaffles. Florence Dibell Bartlett, a Chicago heiress and folk art collector, held the mortgage on the ranch and took possession of the buildings and surrounding seventy-five acres. Bartlett, whose older sister, Maie Bartlett Heard, cofounded the Heard Museum in Phoe-nix, had already built her two-story home, El Mirador, on the ranch property. She continued to spend her summers there for many years. She founded the Museum of International Folk Art, which opened to the public in 1953, not far from Wheelwright's museum in Santa Fe.

Carol Stanley walked away from San Gabriel with her clothes, some per-sonal items, and the cherished baby grand piano that Pfaffle had given her for their anniversary in 1918. But that was not all. Carol also had an important doc-ument in her pocket. Legend has it that the wayward Pfaffle had won a deed to some ranchland near Abiquiú in a poker game, and Carol quickly pounced on it and put the land in her name. No matter how the transaction came about, in the final settlement, Carol owned more than sixteen thousand acres of ranchland that had been part of a land grant given to Pedro Martín Serrano by the king of Spain in 1766. Over time, the ranch had been known by several names, includ-ing Rancho de los Brujos, Ranch of the Witches. The name Carol settled on was Ghost Ranch.

Carol moved to the property along with about a half dozen of the cowboys who had faithfully served the public and all sorts of fancy guests at San Gabriel Ranch. Some of them had even worked for her when the Pfaffles were at Bishop's Lodge. They all took up residence in tents until buildings were erected. Ted Peabody, who had overseen the Los Luceros renovation, was the contractor. He drew up some plans, put together a crew, and set to work making adobes and building casitas.

Hopeful that she could build a guest ranch as successful as San Gabriel had been, Carol Stanley worked hard to make Ghost Ranch into a prime retreat for the rich and famous. From the start, she found she was unable to bring in enough income to cover the expenses and turn even a modest profit. She never got out of the red until she quietly partnered with one of her wealthy guests, Arthur Newton Pack, a writer and the publisher of *Nature Magazine*. Pack adored Ghost Ranch as much as O'Keeffe did, and his infusion of cash and the recruitment of his wealthy friends as guests helped to turn things around. Pack moved his family to Ghost Ranch, and in 1935, he bought out Carol Stanley's interest for $75,000.

Carol married one of her ranch hands, Lloyd Miller, a former professional mountain-lion hunter and a wrangler of dudes at the San Gabriel. The couple then used $50,000 from the Ghost Ranch sale to buy the Cottonwood Ranch, a small ranch close to Los Luceros in the Río Grande valley. They started to breed and train quarter horses, but the economy was still sluggish because of the Depression and Miller's habitual gambling took a heavy toll. Facing foreclosure once again, Carol sold the ranch and all she owned, including the piano. She and Miller left New Mexico and moved to a small two-room adobe outside Arboles, Colorado. Miller ran a feed store, and Carol worked at the post office. She never returned to New Mexico. In 1948, she died of heart failure.

Life at Ghost Ranch was far better for O'Keeffe. She did not miss the social life of Taos or the parties at her friend Marie Tudor Garland's H & M Ranch, and she definitely had no interest in what she considered the artistic incest of Santa Fe. She preferred the isolation and solitude of Ghost Ranch.

In 1937, O'Keeffe arrived unannounced and found her usual casita taken and every bed on the ranch occupied. She was not pleased and told Pack to evict a guest at once so that she could unpack and begin painting. Instead, Pack came up with a more diplomatic solution. Anguished over his wife's suddenly running off with their children's tutor and eager to escape the sad memories of his family home, Pack was moving into what was called the Ghost House where Carol Stanley had lived. That meant that his home, Rancho de los Burros, was available, and without a moment's hesitation, O'Keeffe moved in. "As soon as I saw it, I knew I must have it," she later said.

In 1939, O'Keeffe was unable to go to New Mexico. Instead, she went to Hawaii, where the Dole Company commissioned her to produce a pair of paintings to promote its pineapple business. Neither Dole nor the artist was pleased with the results. O'Keeffe returned to New York in ill health, but by the spring of 1940, she was ready to return to the land she loved.

Once again, O'Keeffe failed to let the staff know she was coming. She arrived to find that Rancho de los Burros was already rented. Pack pointed out that her visit was unexpected. Then the solution to the problem became obvious. She told Pack the problem could be avoided in the future if he would sell her the house. Pack gladly concurred, and for a price thought to be between $2,500 and $6,000, the sale of Rancho de los Burros and eight acres of land was finalized in October 1940.

That fall was when O'Keeffe and Maria Chabot met at Los Luceros and appeared to genuinely like each other. Perhaps as a compatibility test, O'Keeffe invited Chabot to join her on a road trip several weeks after their second encounter at Ghost Ranch. With Chabot in the driver's seat, they took Route 66 to Gallup and then went north to the Chuska Mountains to attend a traditional Navajo healing ceremony. En route and on the return trip, they stopped in the Bisti Badlands, an expanse of sand mounds and eroded rocks hidden away in the high desert not far from Chaco Canyon. O'Keeffe had visited the site before. She called it the Black Place and said in her studio book *Georgia O'Keeffe* that the stretch of black hills resembled "a mile of elephants." It was one of O'Keeffe's favorite painting sites, and over the next several years, she and Chabot often camped there.

When they returned from their road trip, O'Keeffe went to Ghost Ranch to ready herself to go back to Stieglitz in New York. Chabot returned to Los Luceros to do some writing before she left in mid-December to spend the winter in San Antonio. But before either of them departed, O'Keeffe, impressed by Chabot's hard work and attentiveness during their road trip, offered her a job. For room and board and a place to write, Chabot became O'Keeffe's housekeeper, driver, and camping companion. Her duties would include chopping firewood, carpentry, canning, tending flowerbeds and gardens, laundry, organizing camping trips, and whatever else O'Keeffe wanted done. Chabot quickly accepted. She would start in the spring of 1941. That turned out to be just a few months before Pearl Harbor and America's entry into World War II.

"I was a big strong girl," Chabot was quoted by Sharon Niederman in the *Santa Fe Reporter* in 1992. "I didn't want to contribute to the war; I wanted to contribute to art in some way. I was of more use taking her on her painting trips than going out to California to be Rosie the Riveter."

Chabot periodically lived with O'Keeffe at Ghost Ranch and later at Abiquiú between 1941 and 1949. Over those years, the two women formed what one O'Keeffe biographer described as a "tempestuous" friendship. It also was far from being a relationship of equals. O'Keeffe always let it be known that she was the employer and Chabot the employee. On one occasion, O'Keeffe referred to Chabot as "the young woman who lives with me and keeps my world going."

It was long rumored that the two women were lovers. Chabot was intimately involved with females but also had the occasional boyfriend and was briefly married in 1961. She vehemently denied that there was ever any sexual aspect to her relationship with O'Keeffe. Yet it was also obvious that Chabot was totally obsessed with O'Keeffe and displayed fits of jealousy whenever anyone else showed any interest in her. Working for O'Keeffe was much more than a job in the mind of Maria Chabot.

Like O'Keeffe, Chabot did not live full-time in New Mexico during the 1940s and 1950s. She spent the winter and spring months each year attending to her aging parents in San Antonio. During the periods when they were apart, O'Keeffe and Chabot kept up a steady stream of correspondence. There were so many letters offering insight into their relationship and details of their lives that in 2003, the Georgia O'Keeffe Museum in Santa Fe produced a book filled with much of the O'Keeffe-Chabot correspondence from 1941 to 1949. Some of the most revealing of the hundreds of letters are from the later years of the O'Keeffe-Chabot association, when their friendship had become even more strained and contentious than in the past.

The main problem was Chabot's possessiveness of O'Keeffe. A good example was the summer of 1944 at Ghost Ranch. O'Keeffe's casa was besieged with people for weeks. One guest brought her teenage children, and for a while, there was even an infant in residence. So many guests and friends, including Mary Wheelwright, showed up that Chabot quickly grew weary of constantly driving to Martin Bode's mercantile store in Abiquiú or even as far as Española or Santa Fe for food and supplies. Then there was all the meal planning, cooking, cleaning, and dealing with overworked plumbing. As the summer wore on, Chabot became resentful and jealous. She believed the continual stream of people interfered with O'Keeffe's work as well as her own personal time with O'Keeffe. Chabot's anger and jealousy exploded into "tantrums," as O'Keeffe described the emotional eruptions.

Throughout this period of discontent, Chabot found comfort by writing to Stieglitz in New York. In some letters, she enclosed photographs—snapshots of O'Keeffe's two paintings of the Black Place and a painting of a pelvis bone that she managed to complete before she returned East in the fall. The photo that pleased Stieglitz the most was one Chabot took of O'Keeffe perched behind landscape artist Maurice Grosser on his 1938 Harley-Davidson Knucklehead motorcycle. Of all the guests at Ghost Ranch, Grosser raised Chabot's hackles the most. He was the first to arrive and the last to leave. Chabot also felt that he fawned way too much over O'Keeffe. Stieglitz dutifully responded to Chabot's letters, thanking her for the pictures and news from the Far Away, O'Keeffe's name for New Mexico.

At Ghost Ranch, O'Keeffe was not in a conciliatory mood. She could no longer abide Chabot's antics, particularly her rude treatment of Grosser. In October, before Chabot delivered O'Keeffe to the train depot at Lamy for her return to

New York, Chabot was told that she was out of a job and needed to leave Ghost Ranch. Chabot sadly realized she had gone too far. She bore the responsibility for her exile and accepted O'Keeffe's decision or at least appeared to accept it.

After O'Keeffe's train left the Lamy station, Chabot went to Santa Fe to buy a bus ticket for her annual pilgrimage to Texas. She was walking through the Plaza when Staples, Wheelwright's chauffeur, found her. He had been sent to invite Chabot to spend the weekend at Los Luceros. Chabot agreed to go. On her arrival in the early evening, she joined Wheelwright for dinner and a visit in the Grand Sala.

Wheelwright was excited and went straight to the point. Sitting in a high-back chair with a Lhasa Apso in her lap and the rest of the pups sleeping at her feet, she asked Chabot to return to Los Luceros and make it her home. But Wheelwright did not stop there. She further explained that she wanted Chabot to take over management of the property and eventually own it. Later, and with sparse elaboration, Wheelwright recorded her memory of the moment in an undated typescript. "After I had been living in Los Luceros for twenty odd years," Corrine P. Sze quotes Wheelwright as saying, "I invited Maria Chabot from San Antonia [*sic*], Texas to take charge of the Ranch and manage it if possible for her own benefit. I

Sala on the second floor of Casa Grande with fireplace decoration painted by Olive Rush, Los Luceros, ca. 1935. Mary Cabot Wheelwright Collection, Album XVI, Wheelwright Museum of the American Indian, Santa Fe.

hoped that she would be able to make a living from the land as she had a great love of the country and had always wanted to experiment with a ranch."

Years later, Chabot also made note of the unforgettable meeting with Wheelwright in an undated chronology that she likely prepared for some legal matters involving Los Luceros. Although the document lacks detail, Chabot made it clear that what Wheelwright offered was not just a job but a real opportunity.

On October 14, 1944, Miss Wheelwright again asked me to the ranch for the express purpose of telling me that she had been making her will, "And in it I am giving you all of this place . . . everything." Her previous legatee, a cousin, Miss Lucy Cabot, had died the preceding summer. I agreed to make Los Luceros my home and to begin working the land in the spring of 1945 with the assistance of her three male employees. I was sent to Mr. J. O. Seth, her attorney, for his certification of this matter.

—MARIA CHABOT, CORRESPONDENCE IN THE LUCY COLLIER COLLECTION

Unknown photographer. *View towards the East - Badlands*, undated. Maria Chabot Papers, 1866–2002, undated. Georgia O'Keeffe Museum. Gift of Maria Chabot [2013.2.4].

That statement of fact written many years later provides some context but comes off as coldly detached and lacking the mix of emotions that Chabot must have felt. Chabot's letter to O'Keeffe, written that evening after retiring to a guest room at Los Luceros, was far more expressive and detailed. According to Chabot, Wheelwright had told her the following:

> She had made out her will leaving all of Los Luceros to me. I was kind of weak in the stomach listening to her—the luck of it! And then she was crying, saying [that she] "hoped I wouldn't mind," [that she] didn't want it "to be a millstone around my neck," that I could sell it for at least $60,000—or rent it or do anything I wished—only that I must be free with it. I was overwhelmed by tears. . . . She is quite willing for me to make it pay. I told her that I would try to start putting it into alfalfa next summer. There are 130 acres, Georgia, 80 of [them] the richest soil in the valley.
>
> —MARIA CHABOT, IN *MARIA CHABOT–GEORGIA O'KEEFFE CORRESPONDENCE,* *1941–1949*

During the winter, Chabot in San Antonio and O'Keeffe in New York continued to exchange letters, and O'Keeffe continually encouraged Chabot to make the most of the opportunity that awaited her at Los Luceros. In her letters, Chabot frequently expressed misgivings about moving to Los Luceros in the spring and regretted that she would not be with O'Keeffe at Ghost Ranch.

After the holidays, Chabot wrote that she "had unwisely" committed herself to Wheelwright's offer and she was not at all interested in farming. She instead wished to continue writing a book about New Mexico that would, of course, contain much about Georgia O'Keeffe.

Chabot was very much conflicted, but she felt that she had at least to attempt to manage the Los Luceros property. At her comfortable family residence in San Antonio, she looked forward to the latest issues of *The Atlantic Monthly*, but she also pored through copies of the *Progressive Farmer* and read books about animal husbandry, poultry, and other agrarian subjects.

While coming to grips during her time in Texas with the possibility of life as a farmer, Chabot helped to tend the spacious yard. After mowing the broad lawns, trimming palm trees, and hacking down stands of bamboo, Chabot was sunburned, her legs ached, and her hands were blistered and bleeding. It was a preview of what was waiting for her at Los Luceros, but as spring approached, Chabot longed to be in New Mexico. Even if she could not be with O'Keeffe at Ghost Ranch, she would be close to her. By the time Chabot left Texas on the Ides of March 1945, she was resigned to her new beginning at Los Luceros.

After a few days in Santa Fe, Chabot went to Los Luceros just the day before Wheelwright's return. She was already acquainted with Joe Posey, the caretaker and gardener, and his wife, Mildred Rankin Posey, the housekeeper and cook. They showed her around the property, and she took a walk by herself to the river's edge before returning to Dorothy Stewart's house in Santa Fe. In the morning, after picking up groceries for Mildred Posey at Kaune's Market, Chabot met Wheelwright at Lamy, and they drove to Los Luceros.

At first, Chabot had a bedroom in the Casa Grande, but she gradually moved into the nearby small adobe house, or cottage, as she called it, that the chauffeur, Albert Staples, and his wife, Tina, had used until they retired. For the fourteen years Chabot managed Los Luceros, the cottage was her home much of the time. However, she continued her lengthy visits to San Antonio and attempted to manage Los Luceros from afar. Overseeing the property—demanding enough when Chabot was on site—proved to be even more difficult when living at her family home in Texas.

Still uncomfortable in her new role, Chabot started out farming the land on a small scale. She turned a fifteen-acre pasture east of the Casa Grande into her first alfalfa crop and helped with trimming dead wood in the orchards, repairing fences, and spreading fertilizer.

Los Luceros was the largest property of the 126 farms in the area that used the acequia, the communal water-ditch system that irrigated the fields and served as the lifeline of the community. Chabot was appointed one of three commissioners in charge of maintaining the acequia and joined the men from Alcalde and other nearby farms for the annual cleaning of the ditch. Within a few years, she became the first female president of the commission, and for many years to come, she managed as many as three hundred men and numerous teams of horses.

During the years that followed, I was entirely responsible for the maintenance of the land, hiring of employees, management of her [Wheelwright's] household, and ultimately for the care of most of her private

Unknown photographer. *Maria Chabot at Los Luceros on tractor*, undated. Maria Chabot Papers, 1866–2002, undated. Georgia O'Keeffe Museum. Gift of Maria Chabot [2013.3.6].

and public affairs in New Mexico. She visited the ranch for short periods (usually two months) in fall and spring. For eleven years I received no compensation for these activities other than funds, of varying amounts, sent for upkeep of the property (including farm maintenance and improvement).

—MARIE CHABOT, CORRESPONDENCE IN THE LUCY COLLIER COLLECTION

As hard as Chabot worked during her time at Los Luceros, from her first day on the job, she never stopped trying to get back into the good graces of O'Keeffe and fantasizing about the two of them spending the rest of their lives together. For a time, it looked as though Chabot's dreams might come true. When O'Keeffe returned to New Mexico in May 1945, Chabot met her and took her to Ghost Ranch, and at least a temporary reconciliation was in the works.

O'Keeffe was willing to forgive Chabot for her outbursts of jealousy if she promised to behave and, more important, to help with the restoration of an adobe ruin that would become O'Keeffe's new home.

As much as O'Keeffe loved her place at Ghost Ranch, she wanted a more accessible home with arable land for gardening, a place where her life would be easier in winter. An old hacienda in Abiquiú was tempting, even though it was in pathetic condition. It had been the home of General José María Chávez, and after his death at 101 years of age, it remained in his family. In the 1930s, O'Keeffe had first asked Chávez's son about buying the property. He told O'Keeffe that it could be hers for $6,000, a price she considered exorbitant given its poor condition.

When Chávez's son died and the remaining heirs reduced the price, Martin Bode, owner of the mercantile store in Abiquiú, purchased the property. Bode then sold the derelict house and acreage to the archdiocese of Santa Fe for one dollar with the condition that the church build a parochial school or perhaps a convent on the site. However, no funding was available for the construction of either one, so the house and land continued to deteriorate.

O'Keeffe resumed her effort to buy the house, and after meeting with Bode, she found that he was open to the idea of the property being used for something other than a school or convent. The archdiocese still steadfastly refused all her offers. O'Keeffe learned that what the church really wanted was a community center for the village of Abiquiú. She and Chabot met in Santa Fe with Archbishop Edwin Byrne to discuss the situation. Before they left, O'Keeffe wrote a check for $4,000, a tax-deductible gift to the church. Negotiations continued, and her good deed did not go unnoticed. On New Year's Eve 1945, the archdiocese sold the house and three acres of land to O'Keeffe for ten dollars, ten times the price they had paid.

By the time the purchase of the Abiquiú house was completed, Chabot had become indispensable to O'Keeffe once again. She ran errands for O'Keeffe and constantly dashed between Los Luceros and Ghost Ranch to help out. In return, O'Keeffe invited Chabot to join her on a camping trip and paid for the airline fare when Chabot flew from Albuquerque to San Antonio to visit her mother, who had broken her hip.

When she bought the Abiquiú house, O'Keeffe predictably turned to the ever-faithful Chabot to direct the entire renovation. It was a truly tremendous assignment that would take four years to complete. "It took six months just to get the pigs out of the house," Chabot quipped in a 1999 interview.

In July 1946, Chabot and O'Keeffe were picking up building supplies in Española when word came that Stieglitz was hospitalized in New York after having suffered a massive stroke. There was no time to pack a bag. Chabot drove

O'Keeffe directly to Albuquerque, where she boarded a plane to New York. Stieglitz never regained consciousness. At the age of eighty-two, he breathed his last in the early hours of July 13.

The death of Stieglitz was something O'Keeffe had expected for some time. Now, as his primary heir and the sole executrix of his will, she had to deal with an estate that included hundreds of paintings, sculptures, and drawings from noted artists and a photograph collection of hundreds of incredible images, including, of course, many by Stieglitz himself. O'Keeffe devoted the next three years of her life to settling the estate and spent much of her time in the East. This meant that now more than ever, she counted on Chabot to carry on with work on the Abiquiú house.

During the rigors of rebuilding O'Keeffe's house, Chabot tried her best to maintain the agricultural activities at Los Luceros. To beef up the workforce, Chabot recruited laborers from San Juan Pueblo and the nearby villages of Alcalde and La Villita to work the fields and orchards and care for the animals and chickens. She eliminated some of her own farming duties—and added a bit of income to the Los Luceros coffers—by leasing out a large section of the land to vegetable growers from Colorado.

"I found myself with a farm on my hands and a house to build in Abiquiú," Chabot later wrote, according to correspondence in *Life at Rancho de Los Luceros*. "I lived at Los Luceros and commuted many rough miles. If I hadn't been young and strong and crazy, I wouldn't have done it."

All the while Chabot was taking care of Los Luceros, she also made constant trips to Abiquiú to see that the renovation plans she had drawn up for O'Keeffe's house were being properly carried out. Even after the end of the war, building materials were sometimes in short supply, but Chabot managed to get the job done. She hired local men to create new adobe bricks on site and rebuild the fallen walls. Many of their wives slathered on the mud plaster.

While trying to manage Los Luceros and oversee the renovation work in Abiquiú, Chabot tried to please both Wheelwright and O'Keeffe. It was a challenging and sometimes precarious balancing act. To placate both women, Chabot assured each that she was keeping up with all her duties. "I do not want Mary to know any more about the Abiquiú house than is necessary," Chabot wrote to O'Keeffe, as quoted by co-editors Barbar Buhler Lynes and Ann Paden in their book. "I think it will upset her—I know it will—for me to be working up there. She feels I have more than I can handle at her ranch."

In letters to Wheelwright, Chabot began to refer to her as Honji, or some-times Honjii, and used "Hongi dear" in salutations. It was a variation of *hongi*, the traditional greeting of the Māori natives of New Zealand. In 1941 during a visit to New Zealand, Wheelwright had been impressed with the Māoris and their customs, including their physical greeting called hongi, the ceremonial touching of noses when two people meet and there is a sacred exchange of the breath of life. Chabot adopted it as a term of endearment

When Chabot's ailing father died in 1947, she wrote both O'Keeffe and Wheelwright with the news. Several days later, in another letter to Wheelwright, Chabot wrote about missing Los Luceros. "I long to be at the ranch—to smell the new plowing, to see the cottonwoods breaking into leaf."

At the same time, Chabot's letters to O'Keeffe were all about the work on the Abiquiú house and how much she longed for the two of them to be there together. But that dream would never become real. As she kept up the desperate attempt to appease Wheelwright and please O'Keeffe, Chabot continued to be her own worst enemy. Her latent feelings of insecurity and recurring bouts of jealousy doomed any chance of restoring her rapport with O'Keeffe. After a series of conflicts with O'Keeffe's guests in the late 1940s, a final explosion of pent-up resentment and vitriol from Chabot resulted in O'Keeffe's ordering her to leave the Abiquiú house and never return unless invited. This time, there were no pardons or reprieves. With a greatly curtailed correspondence and occasional rare visits, however, their limited and restrained relationship continued until O'Keeffe's death in 1986.

"Georgia was difficult," Chabot told Sharon Niederman in the *Santa Fe Reporter* in 1992. "I don't think she had relationships. Her whole aim in life was to work. Everyone in her vicinity had to help that work. I helped by doing the hard work that had to be done." That work ethic, Chabot's willingness to do "the hard work that had to be done," sustained Chabot during the ten more years she managed Los Luceros, but it did not pay the bills. Financial problems resulted in a constant turnover of farm laborers and often curtailed maintenance. Despite Chabot's constant effort to cut operating expenses and hold costs to a minimum, she had grave concerns about the future of Los Luceros. In 1950, she was barely able to pay weekly salaries to four to six workers, the ranch station wagon needed fixing, and the tab at a small local market was embarrassingly overdue.

Wheelwright, who owned several properties in the United States and abroad and traveled extensively around the world, was financially overextended. Never interested or involved in her own affairs, Wheelwright had no inkling of the situation until she turned over her financial matters to her trusted cousin Josiah Wheelwright, owner and manager of the Atlantic Electric Company, in Boston. He and Chabot became well acquainted over time through a steady exchange of letters. He became Chabot's sounding board and father confessor. Soon Chabot's letters started with "Dear Cousin Josiah."

In the spring of 1951, Josiah Wheelwright sold off one hundred shares of Mary Wheelwright's General Electric stock to cover her losses. By year's end, Chabot had lowered the ranch's overhead expenses, but salary checks were later than ever. When she filed the ranch's yearly financial report, Chabot explained to Mary Wheelwright that she could not reduce expenses any further, according to correspondence in *Life at Rancho de Los Luceros*. "Every dollar of income received from the land during these years has been returned to it in order to fulfill my aim of making the Ranch self-supporting that I may in time be able to relieve you of its expense."

In response, Wheelwright's letters, many of them sent from exotic ports of call during her world travels, asked Chabot to try to cut costs even more. At the same time, following her cousin Josiah's advice, she sold some of her Northeast Harbor property but used most of the profit for trips abroad. "Of course she could continue to support the ranch if she would drop some other things like the museum, Northeast Harbor, Cosmopolitan Club, book publishing and side trips to Europe or Africa," Josiah Wheelwright observed.

Chabot carried on. She took out bank loans, sold off cattle, and leased pastures for alfalfa. When major flooding from the Río Grande threatened Los Luceros, Chabot, with her arm in a cast after an accident, rounded up twenty men to sandbag the Casa Grande, move the furniture and rolled-up rugs from the first floor to the second, and take all the tractors and machinery to higher ground.

Wheelwright leased pastureland to Chabot at a token fee of five dollars a year. Under the terms of the lease, Chabot made some improvements, such as changing fence lines and building sheds and corrals. At one point, Chabot and Wheelwright considered generating more income by opening the Casa Grande to the general public, much as the British aristocracy did with their manor homes when strapped for funds. They asked attorney Oliver Seth to look into how such an operation might work and recruited some Santa Fe friends to help them design a Los Luceros guidebook combining the history of the property with photographs by Laura Gilpin. After much discussion about the possible liabilities, the alterations that would be needed to the Casa Grande, and how to monitor visitors, the idea was dropped.

For several years, Josiah Wheelwright sent Chabot $500 each month to defray the expense of keeping up the Casa Grande and grounds. In the winter of 1954, Chabot expressed her fear that such an arrangement was no longer satisfactory to Wheelwright. Chabot's concern was that Wheelwright thought the money was being funneled into Chabot's farming activities or her personal account.

"It is not—not a penny of it," Chabot wrote to Wheelwright. "I know that it is difficult for you to understand how $6,000 per year can be spent on the upkeep of a place you use so little, but Mr. Seth understands this. He has a complete record of the expenditures I have made for you. A house and grounds, with the motors and animals such as are maintained at Los Luceros, cannot be run in this day and time for less." Wheelwright immediately responded that she had total trust in Chabot. "I hate talking money as much as you do," she wrote. "I am a coward about it I know!"

Unknown photographer. *Maria Chabot and Trujillo at Los Luceros*, undated. Maria Chabot Papers, 1866–2002, undated. Georgia O'Keeffe Museum. Gift of Maria Chabot [2013.3.5].

By April 1956, no longer able to support herself and meet the increasing expenses of the farm, Chabot advised Wheelwright that she would have to take a job and perhaps live away from the ranch. Wheelwright offered her an allowance of $200 per month and on occasion increased the amount to $250 per month. In 1958, Chabot enrolled at the University of New Mexico, with Wheelwright's encouragement. At Christmas, Chabot spent ten days visiting her mother in San Antonio. Wheelwright resented this absence; Chabot suspected that she was becoming demented at the age of seventy-nine.

In February 1957, Wheelwright sent Chabot a letter advising her of a new plan. She had hired a couple to take over running the ranch. Chabot responded by asking Wheelwright for a deed to the portion of the property that she had been leasing. Wheelwright agreed to this proposal and approved a map reserving for herself the principal residence, 4.747 acres of land, and a right-of-way to the rest of the property, according to Marie Chabot in correspondence from the Lucy Collier Collection.

For once, everyone was happy. Chabot had her independence and most of the Los Luceros land, and Wheelwright had her Casa Grande and just enough acreage for some chickens and a garden. The new caretakers, Amado and Lupita Trujillo, were natives of New Mexico. They looked forward to moving back home from Downey, California, so that their sons could continue their education at the University of New Mexico. The Trujillos were expected to arrive at Los Luceros in the early autumn of 1958, just before Wheelwright was to return from the two-month European trip she planned to take with her poet friend, Abbie Evans, in August.

But Wheelwright never made that last trip to Europe. On July 21, 1958, she died at White Hen, her summer retreat on Sutton Island, Maine, three months before her eightieth birthday. That morning, she had worked in the garden and had written a card to Chabot. After lunch with two cousins visiting from Boston, she was tired and went to her bedroom to read. She fell asleep holding the book, and her ailing heart gave out.

Wheelwright was laid to rest in the family cemetery in Boston. In August, Chabot and other friends held a quiet memorial service for her at the museum she had created in Santa Fe. Oliver La Farge, head of the museum board of trustees, and Franc Newcomb, with whom Wheelwright had worked during those

Unknown photographer. *Ranch for Sale*, Los Luceros, July 1959. Maria Chabot Papers, 1866–2002, undated. Georgia O'Keeffe Museum. Gift of Maria Chabot [2013.3.2].

good years with Hosteen Klah, spoke of their friend and her lasting impact on the Navajo people. Chabot and many others at that ceremony also knew that without Mary Cabot Wheelwright, there would have been no Los Luceros remaining. The buildings would have crumbled into the earth, and the land would have been divided up.

A few days after Wheelwright's death, Chabot wrote the Trujillo family in California to break "the unhappy news that Miss Wheelwright died at her home in Maine, July 21ˢᵗ, and that your services will consequently not be required at Los Luceros." The letter must have shocked the Trujillos, but Chabot was in for a shock of her own when Josiah Wheelwright broke the news to her that just six weeks before her death, Mary Wheelwright had made a new last will and testament.

In the new will, Wheelwright bequeathed Chabot a gift of $5,000 and all the Los Luceros land with an important exception. Wheelwright left the Casa Grande and its contents and the almost five acres surrounding it to the Museum of Navajo Ceremonial Art in Santa Fe. Chabot had always believed that she would inherit the main house and plot of land when Wheelwright died. Attorney J. O. Seth told

Chabot that he had tried to talk Wheelwright out of making this major change in her new will but was unsuccessful.

Chabot volunteered her help to the museum when it was made clear that they wanted to dispose of the house and plot of land. She also was perplexed and uneasy about possible gift and inheritance taxes and other issues she had not anticipated. "Mary's changing her will of fifteen years standing and cutting me out of the main house certainly complicates the matter of selling the place," Chabot wrote to Josiah Wheelwright, according to correspondence in the Lucy Collier Collection.

Chabot decided it would be in her best interest to follow the lead of the museum and sell her holdings as well. The museum put a price of $50,000 on its property, including Casa Grande, "furnished in Spanish colonial antiques." Chabot sought $130,000 for her eighty-five irrigated acres, sixty-seven acres of pasture, and two adobe houses. Immediately, potential buyers came forward, including a group of Albuquerque physicians and several well-heeled individuals with an eye on further developing the property as a guest ranch.

The Christian Brothers religious order expressed an interest in purchasing Los Luceros to use as a retreat, and Chabot gave some of the brothers from Santa Fe a tour of the land and buildings. Unfortunately, their inspection was interrupted, as Chabot explained in a letter to Oliver La Farge. "Five dogs . . . almost took the collars off the Brothers! I had to fight them off with a broom and close them in the bathroom, in order to show the house. Unmade beds and dirty dishes do not help matters." The Christian Brothers continued their search for a suitable property.

By late October 1958, a serious buyer did surface. He and his wife wanted to leave their farm in Maryland and live in northern New Mexico. An old friend whom the man had first met thirty years before told him she knew of just the place. It was exactly what they wanted. The place was Los Luceros, and the old friend was Georgia O'Keeffe. The man was Charles Collier. Now, O'Keeffe and Collier were even. He had led her to the land that she loved more than anything or anyone, and she had returned the favor by telling him that a special place he had first seen as a young man could be his.

After some negotiations, Collier bought part of the Los Luceros property in 1959 for $45,000. He then sought to buy the rest of the property from Chabot. It was not an easy or friendly transaction. Collier had his own appraisal of the property made and came up with a value substantially lower than Chabot's six-figure asking price. The back-and-forth negotiations then began in earnest. Chabot tried to be accommodating. When Collier questioned her lease of some of the land to an alfalfa farmer, she promptly broke the lease. At last, Collier made an offer of $90,000 and when Chabot countered with $110,000, Collier walked away and said he would buy the nearby Cottonwood Ranch. That plan, apparently a ruse for Chabot's benefit, was abandoned, and in July 1959, the Collier family officially took possession of the Casa Grande.

From the start, Chabot and the Colliers were bad neighbors. For almost two years, they argued constantly, each side accusing the other of property infringements, trespassing, open gates, and a litany of other transgressions. At last, the war of nerves ended when the emotionally drained Chabot agreed to Collier's offer of $70,000, from which he refused to budge. Collier wrote Chabot, "Considering that our house breaks up the center of your property, the nature of the soil to the south and west of the house, and the actual acreage which can be cultivated, I am sure that our offer is substantially higher than what anyone else will pay. In addition, of course, you save $3,500 in commission."

Maria Chabot left Los Luceros, taking with her many memories, bitter and sweet, of the land that she had both cursed and loved. For a while, she stayed with friends in Santa Fe and then traveled before moving her mother from San Antonio to live with her in Albuquerque.

On Valentine's Day 1961, Chabot surprised those who knew her by getting married. Chabot wed a brilliant scientist, Dr. Dana K. Bailey, in a ceremony presided over by a justice of the peace at the home of her mother. Chabot and her husband, a well-known radio astronomer, planned to make their home in Boulder, Colorado, where Bailey was affiliated with the National Bureau of Standards Laboratory. But before they could even take a honeymoon, Bailey was sent on a scientific assignment to an Antarctica facility where no women were allowed. Chabot opted to go to Cambodia and see as many temples as possible. The marriage lasted six months and ended in divorce. "We were much better as friends than as husband and wife," Chabot confided to one of her neighbors.

For her many contributions to the Native culture of New Mexico and her help in establishing what became the modern Santa Fe Indian Market, Chabot was named a Santa Fe Living Treasure in 1996. She was proud to see both the O'Keeffe house in Abiquiú and Los Luceros become national landmarks. Maria Chabot died in an Albuquerque hospital on July 9, 2001, at the age of eighty-seven. It was said that she was feisty to the end.

10 The Morning Stars

CHARLES AND NINA COLLIER devoted themselves to Los Luceros. That was apparent as soon as they moved into the Casa Grande. The fifteen years they lived there, however, were not easy. Like everyone else who ever owned or tried to manage the property, the Colliers faced and dealt with a multitude of problems, ranging from acts of nature to the difficulties of maintaining and preserving historic architecture. This led to the protracted transition of ownership of Los Luceros from Maria Chabot to the Colliers. The process was difficult and at times extremely rancorous.

Even so, Nina Collier stayed above the fray. She was a peacemaker, not a warrior. A quietly strong woman passionate about the causes she held dear, she comported herself with dignity and grace. Comfortable in the company of every stratum of humanity, she was sometimes compared to Eleanor Roosevelt, whom she knew and greatly admired. Even Maria Chabot had no quarrel with Nina Collier.

Clearly, one of the wiser decisions Charles Collier had ever made was his choice of a life partner. Nina was born in New York in 1907, one of five children of Lionello and Carolyn Allen Perera. Her father, born in Venice in 1873, immigrated to New York at the age of twenty-one. Only two years later, he established a private banking firm that soon made him one of the leading bankers in the city. He married Carolyn Allen, a young woman from a prominent Manhattan family. She became a patron of the arts, devoting much of her life to a mission of exposing children to music, a calling that her daughter Nina also would follow.

Nina and Charles Collier with their dog Bambino at Los
Luceros, ca. 1960s. Courtesy of Lucy Collier.

Nina majored in art history at Bryn Mawr College, graduating in 1928. She
studied design and architecture at Columbia University and in 1934 earned a
degree in architecture from the Massachusetts Institute of Technology. That is
where Nina met the strong-willed Charles Collier. After studying at Columbia
University, Stanford University, and Antioch College, he ended up at MIT, also
earning a degree in architecture.

It was a whirlwind courtship. Before they finished their studies at MIT, they
were married in New York on October 14, 1933, at the Perera family's stunning
Art Deco town house at 49 East Eightieth Street, a residence that many years later
would become the home of Barbra Streisand.

The Colliers made their home in Washington, DC, where Charles's father,
John Collier, was serving as commissioner for the Office of Indian Affairs (in

1947, it became the Bureau of Indian Affairs), a post he held until 1945. As part of the so-called Indian New Deal, the senior Collier was responsible for ending the loss of tribal lands and enabling many tribes to regain self-governance and preserve their traditional culture. At Commissioner Collier's urging, the US Congress passed legislation establishing the Indian Arts and Crafts Board to promote the economic development of American Indians and Alaska Natives through the expansion of the Indian arts and crafts market.

Nina Collier, whose thesis at MIT was about the culture and architecture at Old Laguna Pueblo in New Mexico, worked for her father-in-law's newly formed board. Besides surveying the broad array of Indian arts and crafts, she played a key role in procuring private funding and educating the public about tribal art. She approached New York's R. H. Macy and Company and suggested that the major retailer host an exhibition and sale of southwestern Indian art. All the art selected was sold on consignment at a hefty markup for Macy's. The success of the exhibition and sale brought to light problems with the Indian arts and crafts trading business that led to an investigation of unscrupulous traders and resulted in badly needed reforms.

Meanwhile, Charles Collier also was doing his part for FDR's New Deal, launching the Soil Conservation Service, a new agency under the US Department of Agriculture created in response to the disastrous drought and soil erosion that turned the Great Plains into the Dust Bowl. The program encouraged farmers to practice better conservation methods, such as preserving natural resources, rotating crops, planting trees for windbreaks, plowing the contours of the land, and periodically allowing fields to lie fallow to renew soil nutrients.

In the autumn of 1935, the Colliers welcomed their first child, Charles Rawson Collier. Over the next two years, they traveled extensively through Central and South America, journeys that ignited their lifelong appreciation of Latin American art. After returning to a new home in Falls Church, Virginia, just a few miles from Washington, DC, Nina Collier took on a new assignment as the assistant to Nelson Rockefeller, appointed by Roosevelt to head the US Department of State's Division of Cultural Relations. The Colliers also were busy on the home front as their family grew. Little Charles got a new brother, Lionel, who quickly became known as Leo, followed by a sister, Lucy, named for her paternal grandmother, and baby brother, George Allen.

The Colliers' interest in architecture and the outdoors led them to hire Dan Kiley, who one day would be known as the leading American landscape architect of the twentieth century. A visionary who would work with some of the most influential architects of the time, Kiley became acquainted with the Colliers early in his career. He never forgot their support and the confidence they showed in him.

There was little time for the Collier family to enjoy their home. When the United States entered World War II in 1941, they joined the US diplomatic mission in Bolivia.

The Colliers and their four children moved to La Paz in early 1942. The next two years were exciting, and the work was fulfilling. They stayed clear of an attempted military coup and found time to learn more about the arts and culture of Bolivia and Peru. When their assignment came to a close, the Colliers left behind many friends, mostly writers and artists. They also departed with one more family member, another daughter and their fifth and final child. They named her Monica.

By the end of the war, the Collier family had settled in a new home in Maryland. They purchased the historic Indian Spring Farm, about eighty miles northeast of Washington, DC. The land had been a campsite for local Indians and later bivouacked French soldiers during the American Revolution. In the early 1800s, a rambling Federal-style stone residence with a slate gabled roof was erected on the property.

Additions were made to the house, and by the 1920s, when the neglected building was deteriorating, brothers Charles J. Symington of New York and Donald Symington of Baltimore County purchased the farm and built a second house modeled after the original structure. This addition featured ten bedrooms, two kitchens, a library, formal dining room, den, and butler's quarters. There was more than enough room for the Collier clan and visiting family and friends.

After the Symingtons sold the farm to Collier, he turned the 850-acre property into a modern dairy operation. Indian Spring Farm became the American Scientific Breeding Station, one of the earliest operations of its kind in the nation. Collier's goal was to promote crossbreeding to improve dairy cows in Caribbean nations, especially Cuba and Puerto Rico. Collier brought workers from Cuba to the farm so that they could observe the crossbreeding process firsthand.

While her husband poured his energy into the scientific breeding program, Nina Collier saw to the needs of their five children and devoted much of her time to children besides her own. In the late 1940s and throughout the 1950s, she was a major force in the performance arts movement in Baltimore and beyond. She set up a series of chamber music concerts and introduced the concept in twenty-seven Baltimore schools. A network quickly spread to other eastern cities, leading to the founding of Young Audiences, a national organization serving millions of children.

In the late 1950s, Charles and Nina Collier were restless and ready for a new challenge. Their sons and daughters would soon be finishing their educations and going out on their own. The Cuban Revolution had crippled Collier's dairy breeding program. The prospect of moving to New Mexico became appealing. It was the land that Charles Collier had always loved and Nina had come to cherish from their many trips to see John Collier Sr., divorced from his second wife and married to Grace Volk, his personal secretary. John Jr. and his family lived in Taos and, of course, there was Charles Collier's old friend Georgia O'Keeffe at Abiquiú.

Once O'Keeffe told Collier that Los Luceros was on the market, the die was cast. The Colliers had been collecting Spanish colonial art ever since their early trips to Mexico and Central and South America, including when Collier was a cultural attaché to Bolivia. Iberian paintings and sculptures filled many rooms of their home at Indian Spring Farm.

As their collection grew, so did their interest in saving and restoring the artworks that were uncared for and unappreciated. They found inspiration in the writings of Pál Kelemen, a Hungarian-born archaeologist and art historian who was one of the first to recognize the importance of Spanish colonial artwork produced in the Americas. Much like the Colliers, Kelemen had been part of several cultural survey missions in Latin America. His two-volume *Baroque and Rococo in Latin America* became one the Colliers' most treasured books. They took to heart Kelemen's chilling warning, "Time for salvage is running out."

Los Luceros changed everything for the Colliers. Given its history and location, they saw it as the ideal place to establish a base of operations for the salvaging and restoration of endangered works of art. With the land and historic buildings, the Colliers had acquired some of the Spanish colonial art left by Wheelwright. Much of the collection proved important to the Colliers, such as *Our Lady of Guadalupe*, a striking painted panel executed by an anonymous artist in the late eighteenth or early nineteenth century in what is now New Mexico. Such objects of art and artifacts, combined with the Colliers' extensive collection of paintings, carvings, and religious statuary, would become the nucleus of the International Institute of Iberian Colonial Art, directed by the Colliers.

The Colliers' collecting trips took them to major cities and remote villages in Mexico and throughout Central and South America. In churches and missions, they found religious iconography and colonial art that had been damaged and required immediate attention.

Many people from the art world had long dismissed Spanish colonial art as derivative of European art. Some critics considered it nothing but "religious propaganda." To convince the church leadership of the importance of colonial art, the Colliers attended conferences associated with the Second Vatican Council, or Vatican II, which opened in 1962 during the reign of Pope John XXIII and continued under Pope Paul VI until 1965. The Colliers also lobbied at the Second General Council of Latin American Bishops, held in Medellín, Colombia, in 1968, attended by six hundred bishops from Latin America.

Just before they went to the Medellín conference, the Colliers made a bold move that further bolstered their preservation efforts. They gave the Catholic Church custody of their entire collection. They also willed Los Luceros to the church.

The International Institute of Iberian Colonial Art was to be associated with the College of Santa Fe, where the institute would establish an international museum of Iberian colonial art, according to John MacGregor in the *New Mexican* on December 17, 1967. The Most Reverend James Peter Davis, archbishop of Santa Fe, announced the filing of articles of incorporation that made the International Institute of Iberian Colonial Art a tax-exempt, nonsectarian, educational organization.

Besides Archbishop Davis, others listed as incorporators were some Catholic priests, a few well-known Santa Fe businessmen, Charles Collier, and Brother Cyprian Luke Roney, president of the College of Santa Fe. A governing board comprised forty trustees, with Brother Luke and the archbishop as ex officio members. The institute also had an International Council consisting of "public and cultural figures of international reputation," as stated by Regina Cooke in *The Taos News* in 1970. It was to cooperate with governmental, private, and church organizations in the former Iberian colonies and the United States in developing programs of education and conservation and in the aesthetic and technical training of officials, priests, curators, and other workers.

Although the demands of the institute occupied much of their time and energy, Charles and Nina Collier were able to take care of Los Luceros. They did what they could to maintain the property, despite great expenses and limited funds. They launched an extensive stabilization of the Casa Grande and constructed reinforced concrete foundations to prevent further settling. They made improvements on the chapel, including the installation of handsome double doors that came from a house in Peñasco. The doors were the handiwork of Gregorio Ortega, a skilled nineteenth-century craftsman from the village of Truchas on the High Road to Taos. In 1970, Los Luceros was listed on the State Register of Cultural Properties.

Charles Collier also took care of the landscape at Los Luceros. He planted thousands of daffodil bulbs on some additional land he deeded to the archdiocese. He hired, fired, and sometimes rehired workers from the area to maintain the acequia and look after the fields and the peach and apple orchards. He planted thousands of dwarf apple trees. One season, after early frosts ruined the crop, he installed what was then a newfangled overhead sprinkler system to protect the buds.

Nina Collier used the small library on the second floor of Casa Grande as her office. As always, she remained an avid proponent of arts education in the public schools. The passion for the arts and the organizational skills that had served her so well as a public servant during the Great Depression and later in Maryland proved to be invaluable in New Mexico.

Shortly after moving to Los Luceros, Nina Collier established Youth Concerts of New Mexico, a nonprofit organization that encouraged performing arts programs in the state schools. It was initially intended to be an offshoot of Young Audiences, Inc., but she recognized the importance of making the concert series affordable for the families of rural New Mexico. Through careful planning and by obtaining grant money and federal funding, Youth Concerts became a viable and successful program. Workshops and performances featuring a range of national, international, and local performers toured schools throughout New Mexico.

Despite their heavy workload with the ranch and the arts and educational programs, the Colliers made occasional trips to Spain and Italy as ambassadors for the Iberian Institute. In 1971, Pope Paul VI gave them a papal blessing during an audience at the Vatican.

The Colliers' children were scattered from London, New York, and San Francisco to Berkeley, Albuquerque, and Chimayó. They were pursuing their careers, fulfilling their dreams, and living their own lives. They stayed in touch with their parents and returned for parties and celebrations in the grand sala and walks in the bosque along the Río Grande.

Nina and Charles Collier's time at Los Luceros ended all too soon. Nina died in 1973. Her ashes were buried close to the chapel. Every spring, some of the daffodils that Charles Collier planted still bloom near her gravestone. A poem by Rabindranath Tagore is inscribed on the stone:

Nina Collier gravesite behind chapel

Your smile was the
Flowers of your own fields,
Your talk the rustle of
Your own mountain pines,
Your heart was the woman
That we all know

Charles Collier stayed on at Los Luceros for a few more years, but life there was not the same without Nina and neither was he. He finally moved away in the late 1970s. He died at St. Vincent Hospital in Santa Fe on April 4, 1987. By then, Los Luceros had already had two owners since his time there and was about to be purchased by a third. Still, Collier died believing that Los Luceros had not been abandoned and that the incredible artwork he and Nina had collected was in good hands. In fact, only part of that was true.

The multimillion-dollar collection was safely stored at the College of Santa Fe. It eventually was donated to the New Mexico History Museum to be housed and exhibited in the Palace of the Governors, the oldest continuously occupied public building in the nation.

Los Luceros did not fare as well. When the Collier era ended at Los Luceros, a parade of owners and caretakers took over the property. They ranged from banks and land developers with dreams of subdividing the historic lands for housing to well-meaning private individuals and nonprofit organizations with good intentions but not enough capital for upkeep and badly needed improvements. Tourism officials looked over the property, and for a while there was talk from local politicians about turning the ranch into a state park, but nothing ever came of those discussions.

A conglomerate of Albuquerque businessmen briefly owned the property. They leased the pastures for grazing but made no improvements to the buildings. Like so many others, they failed to recognize what those early tribal people and Hispanic farmers had known so well. Land cannot just be occupied and used; it has to be cared for and nurtured. And one-of-a-kind places such as Los Luceros can really never be owned. They must be protected and their rich legacy curated.

Yet even in the darkest times, when the fields were choked with weeds and the adobe walls sagged and crumbled, there was a glimmer of hope and promise for the land beneath the eternal morning stars.

Some caring souls did their best to keep hope alive for Los Luceros. One of them was Marie Markesteyn, a Georgia native who had moved to New Mexico in 1979. During an afternoon walk while visiting relatives in the area, she came upon the historic site.

"That's when I first learned that Los Luceros, no matter who the owner happens to be, belongs to the community, and it goes against tradition to keep its community from respectfully enjoying the grounds," she wrote many years later in *El Palacio*. "As I stood in front of Casa Grande, my first thought was, 'There's a Southern mansion right here in New Mexico, made out of mud!' Then I noticed it was empty, and had been vandalized. The carved wooden *bancos* [benches] in the grand sala had been ripped out. The sundial has been taken from the lawn. It had no functioning electricity or running water. Some of the windows were broken."

After making inquiries, Markesteyn and her former husband accepted the job of acting as caretakers for the property and moved into Casa Grande in 1980. "My time living there was one of the most incredible periods of my life," she wrote. "For years, I gave tours, telling Los Luceros' stories to visitors. But I think it's still one of the best-kept secrets in New Mexico. A lot of the people I met who live in this area, outside of the descendants, didn't even know it was there."

Casa Grande at night in winter

In 1982, a Santa Fe art gallery owner, H. Malcolm Grimmer, purchased Los Luceros. He and his wife moved into Casa Grande, causing Marie Markesteyn to find a new home on adjacent property that had once been part of Los Luceros. She has never left. A vigilant and dedicated advocate of the old land grant, she has never stopped fighting for its protection.

The Grimmers came to appreciate the intrinsic value of the historic buildings and land. During their brief tenure at Los Luceros, they tried to make necessary structural repairs and improve the health of the orchards and pastureland. By far, their most significant contribution was initiating the successful nomination process that led to Casa Grande, the chapel, and two other buildings being listed on the National Register of Historic Places in 1983.

Unfortunately, in spite of their hard work, the Grimmers found the stress and expense of maintaining the property overwhelming. They left Los Luceros in 1986 when the First Interstate Bank of Santa Fe foreclosed and the property went into receivership. Once again, Casa Grande sat unoccupied, and the lack of regular maintenance brought on more troubles. The acequia system had not been maintained for many years, and as a result, water flowed freely throughout the property, including the first floor of Casa Grande. Before the bank could put Los Luceros back on the market, it spent more than $150,000 to refurbish parts of the buildings that had fallen into considerable disrepair, much of it because of the acequia flooding.

When Los Luceros was somewhat stabilized, it was listed at a sale price of $1.5 million. Potential buyers surfaced and submitted a variety of proposals to First Interstate. One plan called for subdividing the land for a high-density site for houses or trailer homes. Another interested party suggested the creation of a conference center surrounded by residential housing. Thankfully, none of those propositions was selected.

In October 1988, however, a suitable party came forward who had been waiting for the right time. The offer came from Truman Futch, an archaeologist, and his wife, Ann Chaney Futch, a special education teacher, in the name of the American Studies Foundation, their newly created nonprofit corporation formed to solicit funds to purchase Los Luceros. The Futches' first bid, in late 1987, had been denied when they failed to raise enough money by the time the deadline for the down payment had arrived. The next year, they made the purchase when a loan was arranged through a Denver-based mutual fund after the bank received a letter of commitment from the lender. When the transaction was announced in the October 27, 1988, edition of the *Santa Fe New Mexican*, a representative from First Interstate made one thing clear: "If the money does not materialize, the bank will look for another buyer."

The plan called for the foundation to solicit money for loan payments through grants and by transforming Los Luceros into a living museum for the public. As had happened so often in the past, this proved to be difficult. After the foundation had struggled for three years to maintain the property and fulfill their dream of making Los Luceros into a haven for artistic and historical workshops and programs for the public, the funding never materialized. When the foundation defaulted on its mortgage payments, the funders who had financed the purchase of Los Luceros repossessed the property.

A court-appointed receiver sold Los Luceros to Fred Segal, owner of a chain of clothing stores in Los Angeles, for a reported $800,000 in cash. "I think what I bought was a gigantic responsibility," Segal commented shortly after he had made the deal to Ruth Ryon in the *Santa Fe New Mexican*. Like everyone else before him, Segal had his own special plans for the property. He wanted to transform it into a summer camp for underprivileged children.

Segal made it clear that he had no plans to restore Casa Grande unless he received financial assistance from the state. That seemed unlikely because it was estimated that the cost would be at least $250,000. Only a few years before, in 1988, the New Mexico Legislature had approved an appropriation of $900,000 to buy Los Luceros, but Governor Garrey Carruthers vetoed the bill. In 1992, a measure to provide as much as $1.2 million in severance tax bonds to buy the property failed to pass the legislature.

Segal's plans for a summer camp financed through his nonprofit United World of the Universe Foundation never materialized. However, he left his mark. In 1993, he built what became known as the River House, a comfortable two-story adobe on the edge of the Río Grande. He hired an itinerant wood carver from Texas to cut curious human faces and fanciful sayings into the thick bark of some of the ancient cottonwoods. Over time, many of the carvings were covered by bark as the old trees healed. When Segal sold Los Luceros, he left without doing any restorative work in the buildings, which steadily crumbled.

It was not long before someone else came along with a plan to bring Los Luceros back to its former glory. In late October 1995, Roger Hubert, a Kansas native who had spent much of his youth in northern New Mexico, discovered Los Luceros. Hubert took one look at the towering cottonwoods and the deteriorating Casa Grande and, much like Marie Markesteyn years before, knew he had come home.

As a boy, Hubert had heard stories about Los Luceros from his great-uncle Ted Mackie, who lived in the small community of San Cristobal, just north of Taos. Mackie operated a store and supplied horses for Mary Cabot Wheelwright and several guest ranches. "For all the history echoing through the gates at Los Luceros, I was staggered by the unguarded neglect of this important site when I first entered," Hubert later wrote in an unpublished memoir.

The passionate architectural preservationist and self-described "social archaeologist" made it his mission to protect and preserve the legacy of the neglected land and derelict buildings. Vowing to defend the property with his life, Hubert immediately took up residence to discourage trespassers and vandals who had set fires inside the buildings. He was determined to save Los Luceros, and that meant owning the property.

"For me to purchase Los Luceros would be impossible," Hubert later wrote. "But impossible just means it takes longer. I knew so many had tried, and many with money had passed. I knew there had to still be a way to get Los Luceros humming again. Time was short. I approached the California seller [Fred Segal]. I made an offer and he countered. The dance had begun. By November we had agreed and signed a contract. I gathered every nickel I had and with my down payment I had one year to own and refinance."

While busily keeping watch, hiring local teenagers to help with maintenance chores, and encouraging photographic groups to visit the property, Hubert searched for a financial backer. "Fall and winter blanketed in. Photographers kept coming. I was dealing with the issues of big dollars, while guarding, fence mending, hosting, planting and cow chasing. I was an unpaid caretaker but still a contractual owner-to-be. Time, not care, was running out."

In 1997, however, it appeared that Hubert's dream had come true. Winstar, Inc., a development firm from the Netherlands, set its sights on Los Luceros. Representatives met with Hubert, toured the property, and announced their intentions to purchase Los Luceros.

Winstar planned to divide the property into seventeen lots with the potential for a house and guesthouse on each lot. To appease Hubert and others who knew the historical and cultural importance of Los Luceros, the company promised to protect any archaeological remains and restore the Casa Grande and the five surrounding buildings. Winstar's plans looked good on paper to some people, but not everyone agreed, including the Río Arriba County Planning and Zoning Committee and others with a vested interest in the preservation of such an important site. Lucy Collier, daughter of Charles and Nina Collier, residing in nearby Chimayó, was among the area residents who worried about such a development endangering a vital part of the state's history and destroying more of northern New Mexico's farmland. "I think a subdivision of the kind they have developed takes away from the cultural and historical value of the land," Collier said during a May 28, 1987, public hearing about the issue. "My primary concern is that the house be restored and be made open to the public."

Lucy Collier and others, such as Marie Markesteyn, who had never stopped fighting for its protection, knew that either the state or a well-funded nonprofit group should purchase the land. They also saw the value of the state's declaring the site a state monument and making it available for everyone to enjoy.

That was not to be, but thankfully, neither was the proposal to subdivide the land. Winstar's plans were rejected. Los Luceros was back up for grabs. For a while, it looked as if all was lost. Many had tried to make a go if it and failed, not for lack of dedication but for lack of funds. Then, as often happens, history repeated itself. Just as Mary Cabot Wheelwright literally had ridden to the rescue of Los Luceros more than seventy-five years before, some of her Cabot kinfolk did the same in 1999. New Yorkers Frank and Anne Perkins Cabot, distantly related to Wheelwright, became the proud and enthusiastic owners of Los Luceros. "She [Wheelwright] was a friend and a cousin of my grandparents, and I knew her slightly when I was a child," Frank Cabot explained to Bruce Ross in the *Santa Fe New Mexican*, shortly after announcing the formation of the Los Luceros Foundation, Inc. The family relationship prompted the Cabots to visit New Mexico after learning that the Winstar plan to subdivide the land had been turned down.

"There was a wonderful feeling of peace and tranquility of an earlier time when that portion of New Mexico had yet to experience the urban sprawl that one endures today to reach the site," was how Frank Cabot described Los Luceros to Emily Van Cleve of the *Albuquerque Journal* on May 8, 2005. "We felt the place might just still be salvageable and that it was worth undertaking both for its own sake and for Mary Cabot Wheelwright's sake."

Cabot, a blue-blooded financier and self-taught horticulturalist, was one of the world's leading garden preservationists. He quickly addressed the many problems of overgrown orchards and what had once been beautifully manicured gardens. He also directed the planting of hundreds of cottonwoods in the bosque to prevent flooding. He and his wife assembled a team of architectural experts, master carpenters, and craftsmen who carefully rebuilt the unstable main house, which was in danger of collapse. No expense was spared.

Cabot wisely reached out to various sources knowledgeable about the property and its long and colorful history, such as Maria Chabot. He also commissioned Corinne P. Sze to conduct a major historical study, resulting in *History of the Los Luceros Ranch*, an extensive report completed in 2000. Much of the report was based on interviews and information provided by Chabot, Lucy Collier, former ranch employees, and descendants of some of the families who had once resided at Los Luceros.

Also in 2000, Robert O. Binnewies, who had joined the National Park Service in 1961 and served for several years as superintendent of Yosemite National

Park in California, was named chairman of the Los Luceros Foundation board of directors. In 2004, his brother Bill Binnewies, also a longtime National Park Service employee, was selected as the foundation's executive director.

Roger Hubert, whose zealous and often unorthodox behavior had rankled some members of the restoration team, left Los Luceros. "I and my backer [Winstar] had sold the ranch to the Frank and Ann[e] Cabots," Hubert later wrote. "I knew I was leaving the ranch in the next few months." Hubert departed knowing the future was bright for his beloved Los Luceros.

Santa Fe architect Beverley Spears led the team that put major parts of the Casa Grande back together again. The process was difficult and sometimes dangerous. Once, Spears was talking to a contractor in a hallway when the entire southwest corner of the dining room suddenly collapsed. Fortunately, no one was injured. "The upper floor had basically. . . concrete stucco on the exterior, which needed to be removed to take it back to what it was in Mary Cabot Wheelwright's era," explained Spears to Bruce Ross of the *Santa Fe New Mexican* in 2000. "Removing the stucco weakened the building. In a way, it was a precipitous event—the building was so fractured and weak—but I think that's what triggered it."

To oversee the challenging rehabilitation of walls that were cracked, eroded, and listing from moisture, Ed Crocker, an adobe restoration expert and a leader

Tour group visiting Los Luceros on Halloween

in structural stabilization, was summoned. Crocker, a trained Mesoamerican archaeologist with an extensive background in groundwater development and the preservation of historic earthen buildings, and his team solved seemingly insurmountable problems and stabilized the fractured walls. "They are rebuilding history—brick by adobe brick," said one observer who watched Spears, Crocker, and all the others who did the hard work and got the job done.

In addition to the restoration work on the original structures, Spears's team designed and built the five-thousand-square-foot Placita Visitor Center, complete with a bookstore and gift shop, gallery space, living quarters for a caretaker, and a commercial kitchen for events held there. In recognition of her work at Los Luceros, Spears received the 2002 Merit Honor from the New Mexico Chapter of the American Institute of Architects. In 2005, the property was awarded a Heritage Preservation Award from the Cultural Properties Review Committee, the governing body of the Historic Preservation Division of the state's Department of Cultural Affairs (DCA).

The Cabots continued to make other improvements for several years after the historic buildings were restored and auxiliary facilities were built. A new altar was constructed and installed in the chapel, the once glorious gardens were resurrected, and the Río Grande bosque was cleared of tamarisk, salt cedar, Russian olive, and other nonnative invasive plant and tree species. Thousands of cottonwoods were planted along the river. Each year, the foundation donated the wool sheared from the resident churro sheep to a group of area women who carried on traditional weaving techniques. This continuing partnership with the Española Valley Fiber Arts Center helps to keep alive the fiber arts traditions of northern New Mexico. Through the combined efforts of the Los Luceros Foundation team and loyal volunteers, Los Luceros reclaimed its place as the finest representation of architectural styles and building techniques in New Mexico.

As early as 2005, with the estimated $3.5 million Wheelwright House restoration, grounds rehabilitation, and construction of a visitors center completed, the Cabots were ready to move on to other preservation projects. A hands-on horticulturist, Cabot had founded a nonprofit, the Garden Conservancy, in 1989 to preserve America's most extraordinary private gardens. Los Luceros had been restored to what foundation president Binnewies called "turnkey condition," according to Staci Matlock in *The Taos News*. It was time for a new steward to manage and protect Los Luceros.

When the Cabots put Los Luceros on the market for $2.5 million, several organizations expressed an interest in the property. Early on, it appeared that Northern New Mexico College in nearby Española was the prime candidate. The college's first attempt to get funding appropriated for the purchase was unsuccessful. In 2007, a second attempt looked promising when the college secured more than half the funds needed from the US Economic Development Association. However, a legislative appropriation to complete the purpose ultimately failed, and Los Luceros remained on the market—but not for long.

Fortunately, after almost a year of negotiations, on February 14, 2008, the New Mexico Department of Cultural Affairs signed an agreement with the Los Luceros Foundation to purchase historic Los Luceros. During the formal signing ceremony at Casa Grande, Governor Bill Richardson presented a check to the Cabots in exchange for the deed. "We came to this ranch today to breathe new life into Los Luceros," Richardson told the gathering in the grand sala, as quoted by Tom Sharpe in the *Santa Fe New Mexican*. "The acquisition of Los Luceros ensures that one of the state's most unique cultural resources will be preserved. Los Luceros is a gem and I am pleased to see that it will remain open to the public and its history will remain available to generations of New Mexicans."

Shortly after announcing the sale, the DCA issued a report explaining that Los Luceros would become "a cultural destination with interpretive exhibitions and public access." This was good news for New Mexico and far beyond. A single act ensured the preservation of the entire property, including all the buildings, orchards, and fields. As part of the purchase agreement, certain restrictions were included that required the state to

• protect, preserve, and maintain the historic hacienda residence, together with its historic supporting buildings, in perpetuity, for the benefit and enjoyment of the public;
• protect, preserve and maintain in perpetuity the open irrigated pasture and the scenic and pastoral view shed from the historic hacienda residence south and west to the Río Grande bosque and mountains beyond the bosque; and
• have the financial resources and motivation to maintain in perpetuity the historic buildings and open space for the reasonable enjoyment and benefit of the people of New Mexico and of the United States.

In May 2009, there was more good news when New Mexico governor Bill Richardson and noted actor-director Robert Redford announced plans to conduct a film training program at Los Luceros. It was to be called Sundance in New Mexico, after the Sundance Institute that Redford had founded in Utah. The project was then officially renamed Milagro at Los Luceros, a tribute to the 1988 film *The Milagro Beanfield War*, based on the popular John Nichols novel, directed by Redford and filmed on location in Truchas. The intended mission of Milagro at Los Luceros was to offer job training and education in film and the arts, specifically for New Mexico's Native American and Hispanic filmmakers. While advancing the arts as an economic driver, it would also provide a proper interpretation of the history and architecture of Los Luceros.

Although the project planned by Redford seemed feasible, it collapsed after Governor Richardson left office in 2011. Concerns were brought up about the proposed film institute's infrequent use of the site for programming. Some lawmakers and critics of the program were fearful that the state was not living up to the terms of the agreement made with the Cabots. They felt that "Los Luceros should not be allowed to drift again toward neglect," quoted by Bill Rodgers in the *Albuquerque Journal* from a letter to Governor Martinez, as it had before the Cabots came to the rescue. There also were questions of financial responsibility and the issue of Milagro at Los Luceros not having the necessary insurance to use the site. As had happened so often at Los Luceros, the plan was put on hold.

"It was a great idea, and now we're growing those seeds beyond the connection to film," said Patrick Moore, director of New Mexico Historic Sites in the fall 2017 issue of *El Palacio*. "There are all kinds of new opportunities; we're exploring lots of fronts." That exploration had started early on, despite the New Mexico State budget going into an economic tailspin in 2008, soon after the DCA purchased Los Luceros. Although funds were tight, the DCA took immediate steps to preserve Los Luceros. On-site staff secured and maintained the property.

According to Stephen C. Lentz's 2011 report, very little archaeological work took place before 1981 at Los Luceros. Starting in December 2008, the DCA's Office of Archaeological Studies (OAS) began to monitor utility trenches to gain a better understanding of the property. Many artifacts such as pottery sherds, tools, animal bones, and bits and pieces of glass and ceramics were recovered. Some of the pottery remnants could be traced back to Pioge, the ancient pueblo that once flourished not far from Los Luceros.

In 2012, the DCA commissioned the creation of a comprehensive master plan for evaluating the best uses for the entire property, the *Historic Los Luceros: Facility Use Study*. The planning study, conducted by Consensus Planning based in Albuquerque, included receiving input from all potential stakeholders, community members, and individuals or groups interested in developing the future of Los Luceros. The OAS conducted more extensive fieldwork test excavations in November 2012 at Los Luceros prior to proposed construction projects that resulted from the infusion of federal economic stimulus funds awarded two years earlier. The $1.75 million from the American Recovery and Reinvestment Act was earmarked solely for structural upgrades. Beverley Spears, the architect who had overseen the 2001 restoration at Los Luceros, drew up the master plan to expand and enhance the visitor center by adding a multipurpose meeting room, enlarging the kitchen, redesigning the Plazuela, adding a bathing facility, and altering some existing buildings to provide seventeen sleeping quarters for visitors.

In Consensus Planning's final report, issued in 2013, it suggested three primary options for DCA to follow:

1. Manage the property as a New Mexico State monument or museum
2. Sell the property as is, with deed restrictions in place
3. Enter into public/private partnership for different aspects of the property

A single paragraph in the planning study summed up the feelings of many people about the future of Los Luceros: "With proper funding and investment, Los Luceros has the potential to become one of the state's most significant, multi-use cultural sites; a cultural destination with cultural programming and interpretive exhibits, a retreat center for New Mexico film scriptwriters and directors, a working agricultural farm used for educational purposes, and an environmental laboratory for river and water-shed work are several examples of the possible uses of this property."

In 2014, a business strategy for Los Luceros developed by the Arrowhead Center, an economic development institute at New Mexico State University, echoed the recommendation of Consensus Planning. So did a nonprofit group formed in 2012 called Los Amigos del Rancho Los Luceros. Composed of a variety of people trying to "assist and actively participate with the state or any other entity in the preservation, protection, interpretation and operation of this historic

Los Luceros administrative office

site," according to its mission statement, Los Amigos continues to ensure a bright future for Los Luceros.

As the DCA promotes and preserves this extremely important site, it is encouraging to see people's interest in Los Luceros grow. The annual Los Luceros Fall Apple Harvest Festival attracts locals and visitors from far away. The facilities are used for meetings, weddings, and holiday parties. Sometimes special visitors are allowed to stay for a few days in the River House. Members of camera and water-color clubs enjoy the fields and the bosque. Schoolchildren on field trips tour the Casa Grande and watch the spring lambs at play in the pasture.

And there are some people who dream about Los Luceros. They dream of the old adobe fortress and the big cottonwoods and the river. In their dreams, they see all those who came to this place. And if they are lucky, they hear the song of a coyote, the trickster and seducer that roamed this land before anyone, echoing through the twilight.

Following spread: Capilla de Nuestra Señora de Guadalupe & crabapple blossoms
Pages 168-171: River House on the Río Grande

Bibliography

PRIVATE COLLECTIONS

The Lucy Collier Collection

The Wallis Collection

MUSEUMS, LIBRARIES, AND HISTORICAL SOCIETIES

Bond House Museum

Fray Angélico Chávez Library

Georgia O'Keeffe Museum Research Center

Governor Bent Museum

New Mexico History Museum

Nina Perera Collier Papers, 1950–1972. University of New Mexico, University
    Libraries, Center for Southwest Research

Rawson, Collier, and Harris family papers. Kenan Research Center, Atlanta
    History Center

University of New Mexico Libraries

BOOKS

Ackerly, Neal W. *A Review of the Historic Significance of and Management
    Recommendations for Preserving New Mexico's Acequia Systems.* Prepared for
    the Historic Preservation Division, Santa Fe, New Mexico. Silver City,
    NM: Dos Rios Consultants, Inc., 1996.

Adams, Eleanor B., and Fray Angélico Chávez. *The Missions of New Mexico, 1776: A
    Description by Fray Francisco Atanasio Dominguez with Other Contemporary
    Documents.* Albuquerque: University of New Mexico Press, 1956.

Arellano, Juan Estevan. *Enduring Acequias: Wisdom of the Land, Knowledge of the
    Water.* Albuquerque: University of New Mexico Press, 2014.

Barrett, Elinore M. *The Spanish Colonial Settlement Landscapes of New Mexico, 1598–
    1680.* Albuquerque: University of New Mexico Press, 2012.

Beck, Warren A., and Ynez D. Haase. *Historical Atlas of New Mexico.* Norman:
    University of Oklahoma Press, 1969.

Bernstein, Bruce. *Santa Fe Indian Market: A History of Native Arts and the
    Marketplace.* Santa Fe: Museum of New Mexico Press, 2012.

Chávez, Fray Angélico. *But Time and Change: The Story of Padre Martínez of Taos,
    1793–1867.* Santa Fe, NM: Sunstone Press, 1981.

Previous spread: Bridge over acequia with '57 Chevy pickup owned by Urban Martínez, Alcalde, NM

Opposite: Acequia Madre

———. *Origins of New Mexico Families: A Genealogy of the Spanish Colonial Period.* Rev. ed. Santa Fe: Museum of New Mexico Press, 1992.

Collier, Nina Perera. *A Report on a Community Center, Day-School and Clinic for Old Laguna, New Mexico.* Submitted in partial fulfillment of the requirement for the degree of bachelor of architecture, Massachusetts Institute of Technology, Department of Architecture, 1934.

———. *Title I Projects and Others, Española Valley Pilot Program Research, 1966–67 Preliminary Report.* Alcalde, New Mexico: Youth Concerts of New Mexico Inc., 1967.

Cook, Mary J. Straw. *Doña Tules: Santa Fe's Courtesan and Gambler.* Albuquerque: University of New Mexico Press, 2007.

Craver, Rebecca McDowell. *The Impact of Intimacy: Mexican-Anglo Intermarriage in New Mexico, 1821–1846.* Southwestern Studies Monograph no. 66. El Paso: Texas Western Press, University of Texas at El Paso, 1982.

Crawford, Stanley. *Mayordomo: Chronicle of an Acequia in Northern New Mexico.* Albuquerque: University of New Mexico Press, 1988.

Davis, W. W. H. *El Gringo: New Mexico and Her People.* Lincoln and London: University of Nebraska Press, 1982. Reproduced from the first edition published in 1857 by Harper and Brothers.

Day, A. Grove. *Coronado's Quest: The History-making Adventures of the First White Men to Invade the Southwest.* Berkeley and Los Angeles: University of California Press, 1964.

Deacon, Delsey. *Elsie Clews Parsons: Inventing Modern Life.* Women in Culture and Society Series. Chicago and London: University of Chicago Press, 1997.

Díaz, Josef, and Suzanne Stratton-Pruitt. *Painting the Divine: Images of Mary in the New World.* Albuquerque, NM: Fresco Books, 2014.

Durand, John. *The Taos Massacres.* Elkhorn, WI: Puzzlebox Press, 2004.

Ebright, Malcolm, ed. *Spanish and Mexican Land Grants and the Law.* Manhattan, KS: Sunflower University Press, 1989.

Ellis, Richard N., ed. *New Mexico Historic Documents.* Albuquerque: University of New Mexico Press, 1975.

Environmental Health Consultants. *Upper Río Grande, New Mexico: Rinconada, Embudo, Velarde and Alcalde Watershed Management Plan.* Embudo, NM: Environmental Health Consultants, n.d.

GuideStar USA, Inc. *GuideStar Nonprofit Profile Charting Impact Report: Mesa Prieta Petroglyph Project.* Williamsburg, VA: GuideStar USA, Inc., 2014.

Harrison, Birge. *Española and Its Environs 1885: An Artist's Impressions*. Española, NM: Las Trampas Press, 1966. First published by *Harper's New Monthly Magazine*, May 1885.

Hewett, Edgar L. *Ancient Life in the American Southwest*. New York: Tudor Publishing Co., 1943. Copyright 1930 by the Bobbs-Merrill Company.

Hewett, Edgar L., and Bertha P. Dutton, eds., with appendices by John P. Harrington. *The Pueblo Indian World: Studies on the Natural History of the Río Grande Valley in Relation to Pueblo Indian Culture*. Handbooks of Archaeological History Series. Albuquerque: University of New Mexico Press/School of American Research, 1945.

Historic Los Luceros: Facility Use Study. Prepared by Consensus Planning, Inc. Santa Fe: State of New Mexico, Department of Cultural Affairs, 2013.

Jackson, Hal. *Following the Royal Road: A Guide to the Historic Camino Real de Tierra Adentro*. Albuquerque: University of New Mexico Press, 2006.

Jewell, Andrew, and Janis Stout. *The Selected Letters of Willa Cather*. New York: Alfred A. Knopf, 2013.

Kelemen, Pál. *Baroque and Rococo in Latin America*. 2nd ed. Vol. 1. New York: Dover Publications, 1967.

Kemper, Lewis (photographer), and Gregory Schaaf (author). *Ancient Ancestors of the Southwest*. Portland, OR: Graphic Arts Center Publishing, 1996.

Knaut, Andrew L. *The Pueblo Revolt of 1680: Conquest and Resistance in Seventeenth-century New Mexico*. Norman: University of Oklahoma Press, 1995.

La Iglesia de Santa Cruz de la Cañada, 1733–1983. 2nd ed. Santa Cruz, NM: Santa Cruz de la Cañada Parish, 2015.

Lentz, Stephen C. *A Cultural Resource Inventory of a Proposed New Alignment North of the Bridge over the Río Grande at San Juan Pueblo, and 1.4 Miles along NM 68, Río Arriba County, New Mexico*. Submitted by Timothy D. Maxwell, principal investigator. Archaeology Notes 127. Santa Fe: Museum of New Mexico, Office of Archaeological Studies, 1993.

Lentz, Stephen C., and Linda J. Goodman. *Archaeological Testing and a Brief Ethnohistory of San Gabriel de Yunge Owinge, San Juan Pueblo, New Mexico*. With contributions by Adisa J. Willmer and David A. Hyndman, submitted by Timothy D. Maxwell, principal investigator. Archaeology Notes 102. Santa Fe: Museum of New Mexico, Office of Archaeological Studies, 1992.

———. *A Pan, a Spoon, a Bell, and a Gun: Limited Test Excavations for Facility Improvements at Rancho de los Luceros (LA 37549), Rio Arriba County, New*

Mexico. Archaeology Notes 433. Santa Fe: Museum of New Mexico, Office of Archaeological Studies, 2011.

The Los Luceros Historic Property: A Business Strategy. Prepared for the New Mexico Department of Cultural Affairs. Las Cruces: New Mexico State University, Arrowhead Center, 2014.

Lucero, Donald L. *The Adobe Kingdom: New Mexico 1598–1958, as Experienced by the Families Lucero de Godoy y Baca.* Santa Fe, NM: Sunstone Press, 2009.

Lynes, Barbara Buhler, and Ann Paden, eds. *Maria Chabot–Georgia O'Keeffe: Correspondence, 1941–1949.* Albuquerque: University of New Mexico Press; Santa Fe, NM: Georgia O'Keeffe Museum, 2003.

Marquez, Ophelia, and Lillian Ramos Navarro Wold, comps. and eds. *Compilation of Colonial Spanish Terms and Document Related Phrases.* 2nd ed. Midwest City, CA: Society of Hispanic Historical and Ancestral Research (SHHAR Press), 1998.

Martin, William, and Molly Radford Martin. *Bill Martin, American.* 2nd ed. New York: Vantage Press, 1973.

McGeagh, Robert. *Juan de Oñate's Colony in the Wilderness: An Early History of the American Southwest.* Santa Fe, NM: Sunstone Press, 1990.

Merlan, Thomas. *Historic Homesteads and Ranches in New Mexico: A Historic Context.* Prepared for Historic Homestead Workshop, September 25–26, 2010. Santa Fe: Historic Preservation Division, State of New Mexico, Department of Cultural Affairs, professional services contract No. 08 505 7000 0021, March 2008.

Newcomb, Franc Johnson. *Hosteen Klah: Navaho Medicine Man and Sand Painter.* Norman: University of Oklahoma Press, 1964.

New Mexico Primary Sources from the National Archives, Rocky Mountain Region. Denver, CO: National Archives, Rocky Mountain Region, n.d.

O'Keeffe, Georgia. *Georgia O'Keeffe.* Studio book. New York: Viking Press, 1976.

Otero, Miguel. *Report of the Governor of New Mexico to the Secretary of the Interior, 1901.* Washington, DC: Government Printing Office, 1901.

Parezo, Nancy J., ed. *Hidden Scholars: Women Anthropologists and the Native American Southwest.* Albuquerque: University of New Mexico Press, 1993.

Pate, J'Nell L. *Document Sets for Texas and the Southwest in U.S. History.* Lexington, MA: D. C. Heath and Company, 1991.

Plog, Stephen. *Ancient Peoples of the American Southwest.* 2nd ed. New York: Thames & Hudson, 2008.

Poling-Kempes, Lesley. *Ladies of the Canyons: A League of Extraordinary Women and their Adventures in the American Southwest.* Tucson: University of Arizona Press, 2015.

———. *Valley of Shining Stone: The Story of Abiquiú.* Tucson: University of Arizona Press, 1997.

Price, L. Greer, ed. *The Geology of Northern New Mexico's Parks, Monuments, and Public Lands.* Socorro: New Mexico Bureau of Geology and Mineral Resources, 2010.

[Price, Sterling.] "No. 13. Colonel Price's Report. Head-quarrters Army in New Mexico, Santa Fe, February 15, 1847." In *Message from the President of the United States, to the Two Houses of Congress: At the Commencement of the First Session of the Thirtieth Congress.* 30th Congress, 1st Session, Issue 1 of Senate Executive Document. United States, President (1845–1849: Polk). Washington, DC: Wendell and Van Benthuysen, 1847.

Reily, Nancy Hopkins. *Georgia O'Keeffe: A Private Friendship; Part I: Walking the Sun Prairie Land.* Santa Fe, NM: Sunstone Press, 2014.

Roberts, David. *The Pueblo Revolt: The Secret Rebellion That Drove the Spaniards out of the Southwest.* New York: Simon and Schuster, 2004.

Robinson, Roxana. *Georgia O'Keeffe: A Life.* Hanover and London: University Press of New England, 1989.

Roosevelt, Theodore. *A Book-Lover's Holidays in the Open.* New York: Charles Scribner's Sons, 1920.

Rudnick, Lois Palken. *Mabel Dodge Luhan: New Woman, New Worlds.* Albuquerque: University of New Mexico Press, 1984.

Seth, Laurel, and Ree Mobley. *Folk Art Journey: Florence D. Bartlett and the Museum of International Folk Art; Featuring the Florence Dibell Bartlett Collection.* Santa Fe: Museum of New Mexico Press, 2003.

Simmons, Marc. *Coronado's Land: Daily Life in Colonial New Mexico.* Albuquerque: University of New Mexico Press, 1991.

———. *Spanish Pathways: Readings in the History of Hispanic New Mexico.* Albuquerque: University of New Mexico Press, 2001.

Stark, Gregor, and E. Catherine Rayne. *El Delirio: The Santa Fe World of Elizabeth White.* Santa Fe, NM: School of American Research Press, 1998.

Stegner, Wallace. *Where the Bluebird Sings to the Lemonade Springs: Living and Writing in the American West.* New York: Random House, 1992.

Stuart, David E. *Pueblo Peoples on the Pajarito Plateau: Archaeology and Efficiency*. Albuquerque: University of New Mexico Press, 2010.

Sze, Corinne P. *History of the Los Luceros Ranch, Río Arriba County, New Mexico*. Santa Fe, NM: Research Services of Santa Fe, 2000.

Tórrez, Robert J., and Robert Trapp, comps. and eds. *Rio Arriba: A New Mexico County*. Los Ranchos, NM: Río Grande Books, 2010.

Twitchell, Ralph Emerson. *The Leading Facts of New Mexican History*. 2 vols. Albuquerque: Horn & Wallace, 1963.

Udall, Stewart L. *Majestic Journey: Coronado's Inland Empire*. Santa Fe: Museum of New Mexico Press, 1987.

Van Ness, John R., and Christine M. Van Ness, eds. *Spanish and Mexican Land Grants in New Mexico and Colorado*. Santa Fe, NM: The Center for Land Grant Studies/Colorado Humanities Program, 1980.

Weber, David J. *The Spanish Frontier in North America*. New Haven and London: Yale University Press, 1992.

Weber, David J., ed. *New Spain's Far Northern Frontier: Essays on Spain in the American West, 1540–1821*. Dallas, TX: Southern Methodist University Press, 1979.

Weigle, Marta, and Peter White. *The Lore of New Mexico*. Publication of the American Folklore Society. Albuquerque: University of New Mexico Press, 1988.

Weigle, Marta, ed., with Claudia Larcombe and Samuel Larcombe. *Hispanic Arts and Ethnohistory in the Southwest: New Papers Inspired by the Work of E. Boyd*. A Spanish Colonial Arts Society Book. Santa Fe, NM: Ancient City Press, 1983.

Weigle, Marta, ed., with Frances Levine and Louise Stiver. *Telling New Mexico: A New History*. Santa Fe: Museum of New Mexico Press, 2009.

Wells, Katherine. *Life on the Rocks: One Woman's Adventures in Petroglyph Preservation*. Albuquerque: University of New Mexico Press, 2009.

West, Beverly. *More Than Petticoats: Remarkable New Mexico Women*. Guilford, CT: Twodot, an imprint of the Globe Pequot Press, 2001.

Willmer, Adisa J. *An Archaeological Survey of a Portion of State Road 582 near Milepost 5, Río Arriba County, New Mexico*. With contributions by Erin Tyler, submitted by David A. Phillips Jr., principal investigator. Archaeology Notes 34. Santa Fe: Museum of New Mexico, Office of Archaeological Studies, 1991.

NEWSPAPERS, JOURNALS, AND WEBSITES

Brooke, James. "Conquistador Statue Stirs Hispanic Pride and Indian Rage." *The New York Times*, February 9, 1998.

Byrkit, James W. "Land, Sky, and People: The Southwest Defined." *Journal of the Southwest* 34, no. 3 (Autumn 1992): entire issue.

Cooke, Regina. "Art Notes." *The Taos News*, August 27, 1970.

Dixon, E. James. "How and When Did People First Come to North America?" *Athena Review: Journal of Archaeology, History, and Exploration* 3, no. 2, Peopling of the Americas (2002): 22–27.

Duff, Andrew I., and Richard H. Wilshusen. "Prehistoric Population Dynamics in the Northern San Juan Region, A.D. 950–1300." *Kiva* 66, no. 1, Mesa Verde and the Northern San Juan Region (Fall 2000): 167–190.

Fliedner, Dietrich. "Pre-Spanish Pueblos in New Mexico." *Annals of the Association of American Geographers* 65, no. 3 (September 1975): 363–377. http://www.jstor.org/stable/2561887.

Hartranft, Michael. "Committee Approves Monument Bill." *Albuquerque Journal*, November 16, 1989.

Jacobs, Margaret D. "Making Savages of Us All: White Women, Pueblo Indians, and the Controversy over Indian Dances in the 1920s." *Frontiers: A Journal of Women Studies* 17, no. 3 (1996): 178–209. http://www.jstor.org/stable/3346887.

Liebmann, Matthew Joseph, and Robert W. Preucel. "The Archaeology of the Pueblo Revolt and the Formation of the Modern Pueblo World." *Kiva* 73, no. 2 (2007): 195–217. http://www.altamirapress.com/rla/journals/kiva/Index.shtml.

Los Amigos del Rancho Los Luceros. Mission Statement. https://www.rancholosluceros.org/mission-statement.

MacGregor, John. "Aim Is to Preserve Religious Art." *Santa Fe New Mexican*, December 17, 1967.

Markesteyn, Marie, with Candace Walsh. "The Accidental Angel: A Family Visit Led Marie Markesteyn to the Great Love of Her Life. *El Palacio* 122, no. 3 (Fall 2017): 52–55.

Matlock, Staci. "Water Rights Add Value to Proposed Los Luceros Hacienda Sale." *The Taos News*, May 3, 2007, A-8.

Miller, Michael. "Los Luceros: An Early Settlement Along El Camino Real de Tierra Adentro." *Chronicles of the Trail: Quarterly Journal of El Camino Real de Tierra Adentro Trail Association* 7, no. 3 (Summer/Fall 2011): 8–16.

———. "The Secret Sanctuary: Los Luceros." *El Palacio* 122, no. 3 (Fall 2017): 38–51.

Montoya, Rick. "Monitoring at Los Luceros." *New Mexico Archaeology: The Newsletter of the Friends of Archaeology*, May 2009.

Niederman, Sharon. "The Active, Artful Life of Maria Chabot." *Santa Fe Reporter*, Aug. 12–18, 1992.

Petrakos, Christopher Ross. "'We Would Live like Brothers': A Reexamination of Diego de Vargas' Reconquest of New Mexico and the Pueblo Indian Revolt, 1692–1696." *Delaware Review of Latin American Studies* 15, no. 1 (August 31, 2014).

Rodgers, Bill. "After $2.5 Million Purchase, State Film Property Gets Little Use." *Albuquerque Journal*, April 29, 2012.

Ross, Bruce. "Rancho Revival: Los Luceros Renovation." *Santa Fe New Mexican*, April 8, 2000.

Ryon, Ruth. "Santa Fe Brings Home the Stars." *Santa Fe New Mexican*, January 10, 1993.

Sharpe, Tom. "State to Buy Historic Los Luceros Ranch." *Santa Fe New Mexican*, February 15, 2008.

Stahlecker, Dale W. "Crane Migration in Northern New Mexico." *North American Crane Workshop Proceedings,* Paper 323, 1992. http://digitalcommons. unl.edu/nacwgproc/323.

Van Cleve, Emily. "Restored Los Luceros Reopens for Season." *Albuquerque Journal*, May 8, 2005.

UNPUBLISHED WORKS

Hubert, Roger. *Los Luceros—Morning Star of the Río Grande.* Typescript, n.d.

Life at Rancho de Los Luceros: Correspondence of Maria Chabot, Georgia O'Keeffe, Mary Cabot Wheelwright, n.d.

Swanson, Betsy. Los Luceros Hacienda (Morning Star Ranch), National Register of Historic Places Inventory—Nomination Form. National Park Service, United States Department of the Interior, 1983.

Wheelwright, Mary Cabot. *Journey towards Understanding.* Autobiography. Typescript in the collection of the Wheelwright Museum of the American Indian, Santa Fe, NM, n.d.

Wheelwright Museum of the American Indian, National Register of Historic Places Registration Form. National Park Service, United States Department of the Interior, 1983.

Night sky at Los Luceros

Director: Anna Gallegos
Editorial director: Lisa Pacheco
Art director and book designer: David Skolkin
Composition: Set in Bembo and Whitney
Manufactured in China
10 9 8 7 6 5 4 3 2 1

Library of Congress Cataloging-in-Publication Data available from the publisher upon request.

ISBN 978-0-89013-636-2 hardcover

Museum of New Mexico Press
PO Box 2087
Santa Fe, New Mexico 87504
mnmpress.org

Photographs by Gene Peach unless otherwise noted.